POT
LUCK

POT

LUCK

Adventures in Archaeology

Florence C. Lister

University of
New Mexico Press
Albuquerque

© 1997 by the University of New Mexico Press.

All Rights Reserved. First Edition.

Library of Congress

Cataloging-in-Publication Data

Lister, Florence Cline.

Pot luck : adventures in archaeology

/ Florence C. Lister. — 1st ed.

p. cm.

ISBN 0-8263-1760-X

1. Lister, Florence Cline.

2. Women archaeologists—Southwest,

New—Biography.

3. Indian pottery—Southwest, New—Analysis.

4. Pottery, Ancient—Africa—Analysis.

5. Pottery, Ancient—Spain—Analysis.   I. Title.

E78.S7L62 1997

930.1'092—dc20

[B]

96-10006

CIP

My paean of
joy and thanksgiving
for Bob, Frank, and Gary,
and the potters of the world

Contents

Foreword

In their foreword to *Hidden Scholars: Women Anthropologists and the Native American Southwest*, Nathalie and Richard Woodbury observe that in the past many women were "too often a part of the background of southwestern studies" and rarely gained the prominence of their male counterparts. Florence Lister always has been reticent to take her place among the women and men who have contributed to a better understanding of human history, but this book helps to set the record straight.

Though her contributions are reflected in a long string of books, monographs, and articles, this book differs from earlier works in two significant ways. First, she is the sole author, a role she would not have chosen, but which was caused by the untimely death of Bob, her cherished husband and long-time collaborator. Second, this is a "behind-the-scenes" book that not only gives the reader an understanding of scientific inquiry, but also a good sense of the serendipity that often characterizes good analytical research.

The book has other strong merits. Through a variety of exquisitely drawn vignettes, Florence ably conveys the importance of ceramic studies to anthropology. Her effectiveness in doing so comes from having been deeply involved in essentially every task associated with producing, using, and studying pottery. This is a woman who, among other things, has washed potsherds, analyzed paste and temper, thrown and fired pots, cooked *frijoles* in *ollas*, and compared notes on maiolica production centers with the small set of world experts on that subject (of which she is a leading member). She also rather effortlessly helps us to see how ceramics can serve as an interpretive link between multiple facets of past and present societies. Even more significantly, she uses those interpretive links cross-culturally and cross-temporally. Ultimately, we gain a greater awareness and appreciation of the many social commonalities underlying the apparent diversity of this almost worldwide craft and art. Finally, and perhaps most importantly, this is a personal story that charts not only the growth of an archaeological subdiscipline—ceramic analysis—but also the role played in that process by Florence and her entire family. This is a welcome change from the more common and occasionally ponderous accounts of an individual's research progress.

Florence hinted to me that this might be "the last book." Let us hope not. We need writers who not only have the talent to help us understand the scientific process, but who can also make us enthusiastic about that process. Such talent should be encouraged, but more importantly, treasured.

R. Gwinn Vivian
Arizona State Museum
Tucson

Preface

Archaeology has widespread appeal to its professionals and to interested laymen alike for a variety of reasons. There is a common itching inquisitiveness about humankind's past that can be soothed by analytical studies of recovered tangible goods or evidences of environmental modifications created by former cultures. A pervasive element of mystery-solving gratifies the scientist, and, when properly presented, makes for suspenseful reading by others. Also, the study of archaeology offers an escape from what are often viewed as the unpleasant realities of the here and now. Tune in the past and tune out the present. Never mind that the civilization being considered may have been characterized by daily rampant harshness or even extreme brutality; that for a time its citizens may have barely survived the unrelenting demands of physical and human nature to eventually be forced into defeat by moral decadence, by economic maladjustments, or by needless deaths from disasters, ignorance, or warfare. Time and distance tend to mellow those hard-edged facets of life into an illogical patina of glamour. What is old and removed is transformed not only into what is exotic but also into what is captivating.

Then, there is the universal zest for the gamble and the unexpected discovery. Buried in the unknown and underneath the earth's surface are potential archaeological riches, be they intellectual or worldly. No one can predict with exactness what lies in some little known corner of the globe or beneath its seas, nor even what the next shovelful of dirt will reveal. Perhaps something noteworthy, perhaps nothing. This does not deny expertise on the part of researchers, but merely recognizes the element of chance. Here reactions may vary. One person's excitement for another culture may, to others, be the uninteresting chaff winnowed from a vanquished era. Moreover, monetary value, by which much of the present accouterment of life is judged, can seldom be attached to recovered artifacts. Obsolescence does not necessarily mean worth; however, the dreams of important finds, whether of knowledge or of commodities, persist. This is all to the good because they fuel continued studies. Such interest is evidenced by school books filled with accounts of King Tutankhamen's tomb, Ur of the Chaldees, the Elgin marbles, the Paleolithic caves of southern Europe, Pompeii, Angkor Wat, Olduvai Gorge, or Machu Picchu, and by the world-wide parade of millions of visitors to these and similar archaeological sites and museums. Lacking the great age, huge scale, and overpowering works of art typical of many Old World antiquities, the lesser, more recent aborig-inal remains of the American Southwest have assumed a different allure because they have become an integral part of the lore of the Old West and its visions of cowboys, Indians, and lost Spanish treasure. This perception is more synchronized with contemporary regional life.

Even in this age of impersonal computerization, the pursuit of archaeol-ogy involves a certain amount of on-site research. It is the physical rigors that often go with such activity that excite many of this science's practi-tioners, who find that side of the work far more entertaining than the painstaking mental exercises needed to interpret the retrieved data. Just as for many laymen, however, there are fantasies about the past, and there are frequent stereotypical views about archaeologists and their field expeditions that are rooted in the endeavors of another generation.

Some persons see these scientists as out of touch with reality but always colorful and eccentric. Today they are still apt to be on the fringe of national political and economic life, and they tend to remain social nonconformists. In one traditional picture of them, they don a pith helmet, walking shorts, and knee socks (nowadays wearing a headband, preferably faded blue jeans, and expensive hiking boots), march off into the uncharted wilderness with a platoon of diggers (now likely flown by helicopter or transported by four-wheel-drive vehicle to a well-mapped sector that is about to become a major energy reserve and where a mechanical backhoe may be waiting to do much of the heavy earth removal). There they bed down in a comfortless, tented camp, which is swathed in mosquito netting and has no facilities or contact with the outside world, but which is nevertheless staffed with obsequious servants who produce hot gin from a canteen and cook mysterious foods by native means (no change except for air mattresses, butane stoves, portable toilets, shortwave radios, typewriters, cameras, plane tables, Brunton compasses, insect repellent, ice, and a camp cook who dishes out chili and beans while doubling as a shovel hand working on a Ph.D. dissertation). The removal from the distractions of current problems (meaning no TV, newspapers, or mail), combined with the romance of communing with departed spirits (utter silence in ghostly, snake-inhabited dwellings or mounds); with adventure in faraway places (read this as hardship and second-class travel); and with a healthful life in the open (sunburn, aching muscles, spartan meals, and early bedtimes because of darkness and little else) make it seem an idyllic life to some persons both inside and outside the profession. Those on the outside, however, are prone to question archaeology's value in the real world, code phraseology for "how do you make a living?" Those on the inside scramble for answers as they scramble for financial support. They know that, even if there were no high-sounding rationale for coming to terms with today's dilemmas through an understanding of prior human cultural attainments, they would continue doing what they are doing. Being an archaeologist entails a cast of mind and heart, even a total commitment to a way of life that once adopted cannot easily be put aside.

With no regrets, I have luxuriated for half a century in this archaeological mystique both by choice and by marriage. Some of those on the outside of the profession have urged me to write this account, being, it has always seemed to me, a bit envious. And well they should be!

The rumination to follow has two facets. Its familial side, written in narrative style, tells of some archaeologically related episodes, personalities, and impressions that gave my life its color. In more introspective prose, the serious side concerns my view of ceramics and is dealt with in various professional capacities as a means of cultural interpretation. The two halves meshed to make for a most rewarding whole.

How It Began

In retrospect, I know exactly when I decided somehow to share in that exciting branch of knowledge called archaeology. In the late 1930s my dear father had just returned from visiting a ranch in the Mimbres valley of southwestern New Mexico, where his host had introduced him to the favorite local pastime of hunting pots in a small Indian ruin out in the back forty. While poking around a battlefield of earlier potholes, they had stumbled upon what appeared to be a human burial beneath the dirt floor of a collapsed house. All that remained were a hollow-eyed skull lying askew in the caked earth and some long bones flexed upward into a tight, eternal sleeping position. Lying beside them was a crinkly-surfaced pottery jar, which to judge from the soot still blackening its exterior, had seen much service over an open fire. My father explained that they had not saved it because it had a hole in its bottom and was therefore useless.

My sophomoric curiosity was so piqued by this second-hand glimpse of life far removed from my own that I drove my Model A coupe across Los Angeles at the earliest opportunity in order to spend an entire afternoon at the prestigious Southwest Museum. There I learned that the pot was a kind called corrugated because the encircling clay coils from which it had been made were precisely pinched on the exterior surface. To me, they looked like concentric wheels of pie crust. Moving through the exhibits, I found myself riveted to a display case, in which a magnifying glass was positioned over a jagged fragment of such pottery. Caught in the carefully spaced, pinched depressions were the fingerprints of the artisan, each skin configuration still as sharp as I imagined those to be in any modern police blotter. Indelible and certainly uninten-

*A potter's fingerprints retained forever in the soft clay of a vessel
under construction*

tional, they were a compelling voice sounding across the centuries that sent
my psyche reeling. Who was this potter whose personal signature had been
captured for posterity? Unaware that women were thought to have been these
artisans, I wondered how he had fit into the world around him. As creator of
something both useful and beautiful from the common earth, had he possessed
a special sensitivity? That seemed very probable to me after I read the informa-
tive label explaining that even humble objects such as earthenware were believed by their makers to have inner spirits. If pottery had in fact served as
grave furnishings, as in the case of Dad's jar, then those spirits had been released through a small hole punctured in the vessel walls to accompany the
spirits of the deceased. As the archaeologists coldly put it, the vessel was
'killed'. With that disconcerting thought, I left the museum knowing that I
would forever be attracted to pottery and to the cultural undercurrents accom-
panying it.

Within a short period of time, I devoured a suggested reading list, took an
introductory anthropology course by correspondence, changed my major, and
transferred to the University of New Mexico in the fall of 1939. Along the way,

I happened upon a book by Ann Axtell Morris, *Digging in the Southwest,* which, from a wife's perspective, recounted field work in an untamed sector of the Southwest that offered adventure, intellectual challenge, and downright fun. More than I knew at the time, that book was to have a profound influence on me because I identified with what I saw as an exotic life played out in a supporting role.

In New Mexico I found a stimulating world bursting with amazing natural and cultural diversities, the facts and fictions of long human presence. At that time it was populated by Indians who tried to look like Anglos, by a motley group of Anglo students who tried to look like Indians, and by unconcerned Mexicans who just went on being themselves. Many of the students were the dropouts of their day. The sufferings of the Great Depression had driven them to seek haven in other times and places. Having little money, they defiantly flaunted their poverty by adopting ethnic clothes and mores.

Still entranced by my introduction to prehistory, I chose as my first class one that was devoted to the pottery of the ancient Southwest and taught by Florence Hawley (then Senter). It was a subject for which I was grossly unprepared. I was totally unfamiliar both with the physical geography of New Mexico, Arizona, Colorado, or Utah, and with their strange-sounding place names and provinces that provided much of the proper nomenclature used for the pottery I was about to study. I knew even less about the aboriginal cultural record or its evolutionary stages that scientists had so far determined. To my knowledge I had never met a potter, nor did I have the slightest idea how pottery of any kind was fashioned or finished. I don't suppose I had ever even seen an Indian pot actually being used except to hold a bunch of dried leaves and branches in a non-Indian home. Fortunately, I also was not yet aware of the fact that ceramic analysis and identification were veritable quagmires into which more than one professional had already hopelessly sunk.

But one thing was very obvious to even a novice like myself: This class was certainly no place for fanciful musings on earthen voices from the past. It was instead a no-nonsense exercise in the rapid-sight recognition of several hundred pottery variations, of both minor and major dimensions, to which regional archaeologists seemed to attach spatial and temporal significance. Except for good eyesight and keen observation skills, the only other special qualifications or tools needed for identification was a low-powered hand lens. I did not yet comprehend the distinctions between categories, although on the surface, such categorization appeared to be a dehumanizing approach to understanding the handiwork of the ancients. There were few whole pottery vessels to be seen in the classroom, just banks of drawers filled with fragments. As most uninitiated observers, I wondered how one could ever put them all back together again.

After enrolling in the University of New Mexico, I realized that the science of Southwestern archaeology was still in its exciting youthful ferment. New sites, new categories of artifacts, new perspectives on vanished life ways, and even entirely new horizons of human progression were steadily being discovered or postulated. Many of the stalwart men were still around who had over the immediately preceding decades brought the unique display of local antiquities to popular attention. These were people like Byron Cummings, Neil Judd, Earl Morris, Edgar Hewett, Frank Roberts, Nels Nelson, and Frederick Hodge. Women were in short supply, but those few who were present, along with the men with whom they worked, were rapidly being transformed into colorful folk heroes in the eyes of the next generation—a generation that was longing to follow in their footsteps.

This was all a heady dose for a rank beginner in the study of prehistory, who until several years ago had never considered life in any form east of San Bernardino. Bewildered but buoyant, I somehow muddled through. Because I was then nineteen and from a poor working class family, however, I knew that I could not just drift along on a cloud of euphoria resulting from my personal contact with another civilization. I needed occupational goals to justify my educational expense, and I decided to seek advice on what I feared were only remote possibilities of a remunerative future in my newly found passion.

Dr. Florence, whose ceramic course I had just completed, was a stylish young woman who did not fit the popular stereotype of female archaeologists as weather-beaten slobs. Other persons who assured me that they were on a first-name basis with her, told me of having good times with her at Navajo sings, of sharing hospitality in the homes of her Indian friends, and of her often liking to grill dinner in her fireplace. From these and from other gossipy snippets, it was obvious to me that we were soul sisters, even to the point of sharing the same given name. I therefore decided to go to her office for a woman-to-woman chat.

Dr. Florence assured me that it was indeed a tough, man's world out there

in Southwestern archaeology. She implied that she felt tinged by some resentment. The only way to break into the discipline, she confided, was to find
some aspect of the work that men did not enjoy doing and then to become a
specialist in it. In the days of acquiescence before strident women's liberation
appeared on the scene, that seemed a reasonable suggestion. As I intently listened to this ceramic expert who obviously had succeeded and then recalled
that a co-author of the first archaeological report I had ever read was another
female named Hattie Cosgrove, also known for her knowledge of regional pottery, I was slowly but surely becoming committed to a lifelong love-hate relationship with potsherds. Just to ensure myself of a possible solvent future, however, I decided to secure a teaching certificate through the College of Education,
aiming, if all else failed, to work for the Indian Service.

The next summer I had my first taste of what it would be like to be a part of
the archaeological scene when I enrolled in the university's field school at Chaco
Canyon National Monument. There in the bleakness of northwestern New
Mexico, amid one of North America's most impressive concentrations of ancient ruins and surrounded by the eastern extension of the far-flung Navajo
Reservation, the Anthropology Department spent half of each summer expos-
ing cadres of neophyte diggers to the demands of practical field work. We
were housed in quarters modeled after Navajo hogans because even the university architects were caught under the spell of native culture.

The schedule called for dividing the work day between learning field methods at a small Anasazi (ancestral Pueblo) dwelling nearby during the early morn-
ings and late afternoons and attending lectures during the heat of midday. In
a short period of six weeks, these classroom sessions provided us with an overdose of anthropological information. Florence Hawley Senter, Paul Reiter, and
Frank H. H. Roberts, all of whom had learned many of their archaeological ropes
in Chaco Canyon, steered a course for us through the murky seas of Southwestern prehistory as it was then understood. Added to that background were
lectures on a variety of subjects including Peruvian, Mayan, and northern Mexican archaeology; ethnobotany; Navajo culture and entomology; and the Spanish Colonial history of New Mexico. Lecturers included resident or visiting
scholars such as George Hammond, Donald Brand, J. Eric Thompson, Julio
Tello, E. F. Castetter, W. W. "Nibs" Hill, Clyde Kluckhohn, and Leland Wyman.
Sitting in a hot room right after lunch, we soon realized that our greatest chal-

Florence at Peñasco Blanco, Chaco Canyon, 1940

lenge was trying to keep from dozing while Ernst Antevs, in his peculiar mutation of English and Swedish, expounded on the geological past of the Southwest.

Sandwiched in-between these academic exercises were excursions to Navajo ceremonies, visits to the canyon trading post, exploratory hikes, group sports, and general camp horseplay. For me, the wrecked but handsome structures standing in silent formation before the tawny cliffs still reverberated with lingering forces of the human drama that had come to an end there over eight hundred years earlier. This was the romance of archaeology that was enjoyed by the intellectually immature such as myself, but was repelling to hard-nosed scientists who were determined to erase the stigma of subjectiveness from their discipline.

For me, however, another, more meaningful, romance was in the offing. One ruddy twilight near the end of the field work season, I sat with some girlfriends on a wall stub idly watching both a raucous horseshoe game in progress and a young Park Service ranger trotting up the road toward us. I had seen the runner around camp several times during the summer, but we had not yet met. He stood out because of his confident cheerfulness and his dark good looks. I asked my friends who he was. They looked at me in utter astonishment. "Why, that is Bob Lister," they chorused. Obviously, Bob Lister had admirers who, as it turned out, were anticipating his being on campus during the coming year to teach some anthropology classes while Professor Donald Brand was on sabbatical. That was interesting news. I had not forgotten another piece of advice from Dr. Florence, and for a fleeting moment, I wondered about the truth of predestination. While commenting on the gender bias of her profession and how I might surmount it, she had turned to me and quite seriously said, "Your best bet is to marry an archaeologist!"

That remark was not a frivolous comment for the time. The activities and shared interests of the small department set the stage for a number of marriages within the ranks. Dr. Florence had married Donovan Senter, a graduate student. My bunkmates were planning unions of their own—Gretchen Chapin with Alden Hayes and Carolyn Miles with Douglas Osborne. The upcoming war would hasten half a dozen other pairings. Perhaps my turn would also come.

To comply with camp rules, one day near the end of the session, I stopped at the Park Service office to report a planned excursion. I had borrowed a girl-friend's car intending to drive to the western end of the canyon over the faint old wagon track, park, and climb to the Pueblo great house of Peñasco Blanco that bulked on the crest of the southern mesa. The man in the office to whom I spoke was Gordon Vivian, a government archaeologist of whom I had heard but never met. As I was leaving and out of earshot, Vivian turned to an assistant and with resignation moaned, "Well, we're going to have to dig *her* out!"

Within half an hour, I was as thoroughly embedded in the deep sandy ruts as some Pleistocene monster in the oozing La Brea tar pits of my hometown. Pushing stubborn prickly greasewood under the wheels did not solve my problem, which only seemd to get worse the more I attempted to maneuver the car back and forth. Thoroughly frustrated, there was nothing I could do but hike back the four miles to the office in the July heat and humbly ask for help, knowing that this embarrassing incident would certainly confirm the prevailing opinion of the male staff there that females had no damned business in this guys' game.

Shortly thereafter back at school, I secured two student jobs in order to help meet expenses. At night I was proctor at the women's dormitory, and for several afternoons a week, I typed for Professor Leslie Spier. I had previously taken Spier's class on the ethnography of the native tribes living in the lower Colorado and Gila river valleys. Spier was the current authority on this subject, but I found the topic and presentation to be as dry as the environment in which those people had lived. Naturally I did not divulge these feelings to the professor because professionally, he was at the top of the departmental hierarchy, and I felt honored to be associated with him even in such a menial way.

Dr. Spier set me up in the corner of his office at a table that was stacked with sheets of paper full of thousands of carefully handwritten but incomprehensible words lacking any punctuation signposts. It was part of a linguistic text that was being prepared for publication, that made no sense to me, and that was exceedingly difficult to transcribe on a large manual typewriter. I very much wanted to produce an errorless copy, but the going was painfully slow and disquieting. If this was the kind of research that ethnologists had to do, I thought to myself, then regional archaeologists could consider themselves fortunate in not having to interpret either written or oral language because none was known for the ancient inhabitants of the northern Southwest. Typing potsherds surely must be easier and more satisfying.

My timidness at work was heightened by Spier's unsmiling reserve. He openly took exception to the freewheeling informality that characterized most departmental relationships. It offended his New York standards of academic propriety. His office door was therefore shut while all others along the hall stood open. His office hours were posted, and students and staff alike had best observe them. One knocked, waited for a response, entered, briskly stated the business at hand, and departed. There was no idle chitchat, no overstepping of bounds, no friendly gesture. Added to this rigidity was an almost priggish devotion to order, which I suspected came from his early training as a civil engineer. Books were properly upright on their shelves. Notes were piled and neatly identified. Pencils were sharpened and placed in rows. There were no thoughts scribbled on paper scraps scattered about the desk. Compared to what I knew were the usual conditions in the adjoining offices, it was hard to see that work was being done at all in Spier's domain. I could testify that it was, however, even though my snail's pace threatened its completion and order steadfastly prevailed.

During the following summer at the Chaco field station as I watched Dr. Spier diligently policing the grounds with a stick, which had a nail protruding from one end and with which he was stabbing stray cigarette butts, my judgment of him as a soulless martinet seemed to be confirmed. Did he notice the glorious sunset that stained the sky at the western end of the canyon? Did he thrill to a coyote's nighttime wail or laugh at a group joke? Alas, when he unexpectedly sent me a kind note a year later congratulating me on my upcoming marriage, I belatedly realized that I had blindly missed a rare opportunity. Given the unstated but mutually recognized social barriers, we never could have been easy friends, but I need not have been intimidated for months by Spier's stern exterior.

After the 1941 graduation ceremonies, which were held out of doors in a grove near the old Rodey Hall and at which I was surprised to receive a *magna cum laude* designation, I took on the task of helping to run the ceramic lab at the Chaco field school. It was my first solo attempt at classification of material that encompassed thousands of specimens, and since pottery studies in general were relatively unplowed turf, there were few established standards with which to work. As I sat before the small hillocks of potsherds that grew like weeds on the work tables and spilled over onto the lab floor, I experienced a feeling that I was to know repeatedly during subsequent years. Although a roomful of pottery inviting explanation held an irresistible fascination for me, I also felt a depressing sense of being overwhelmed by a mass of inarticulate artifacts that seemed to defy categorization. Maybe linguistic studies were not so bad after all.

As my familiarity with specimens grew, however, I saw that the order necessary for understanding them could replace the seeming chaos. It was amazing to me that based simply upon visual characteristics, the bulk of thousands of earthenware pieces that had been produced over several centuries could be segregated into no more than half a dozen groupings, each one distinctly formed or decorated within a very limited range of acceptability. It was this same kind of conservatism of spirit that had also typified other aspects of Pueblo culture. Nevertheless, it was also reassuring that human individualism had survived, since there was a frustrating handful of samples that did not fit into these pigeonholes. Over in a corner, a sand table held a dozen vessels in various stages of reassembly. Never having been adept at puzzles, I found this job a perplexing one that sorely tried my patience, but the insight these vessels provided for a fuller description of the types was essential.

There was another, more prosaic side to my chosen science, as I quickly learned in the lab during that summer of 1941—that of drudgery. There were no blisters, no sunburns, no encounters with rattlesnakes, and no unanticipated finds revealed under a troweling. There was just tedium. No wonder the men let the women handle pottery processing! All the thousands of fragments, both large and small, that were coming out of the digs had to be washed in order to get a clear view of their characteristics. Sometimes this meant an additional weak acid bath in order to remove mineral incrustation or discoloration. After drying came the provenience labeling with indelible ink. This included not only site reference but also the exact position and depth of recovery. The next task of gross sorting by stylistic type was even more challenging. This statistical information, which was achieved at that time with paper, pencil, eraser, and fortitude, but without electronic aids, would be relevant in interpreting the age of the site, in determining the probable kinds of utilization for particular parts of the settlement, and possibly even in comparing the economic status of the occupants.

I found that it was the ceramic technician's lot to work primarily with fragments that could not be reassembled. The exceptions were the times when a vessel had been crushed where it had been abandoned by the weight of the drifted fill that covered it or by the roots of plants that later grew in that covering mantle. I knew of one outstanding deposit of 112 particularly fine cylindrical jars that had been recovered at the largest Chaco town of Pueblo Bonito directly across the canyon, but nothing that spectacular was uncovered in the village that was being dug that summer. One advantage in working with potsherds, however, was that the inner cores of the wares were exposed, thus permitting the kinds of physical examinations impossible with complete vessels.

Analysis of the Chacoan decorated wares required most of my attention. Because the sites that were being opened that summer by the student excavators and the Navajo laborers were small villages representative of a period the archaeologists regarded as Pueblo III—or the climactic final phase of Chaco occupation—these types typically bore a chalky white slip and flat black geometrical designs that were dominated by finely lined diagonal hatchures, serrated triangles, scrolls, and dots. Especially abundant among the utility wares were fragments of the same kind of corrugated cooking pots that had started my involvement in Southwestern archaeology. I now realized that their roughened surfaces made them easier to grasp during daily chores, and, as others had pointed out, perhaps the many surfaces created by the pinching technique helped to distribute and retain the heat of the cooking fires. The shapes usually indicated for both decorative and cooking wares were pitchers, serving and cooking bowls, water and storage jars, ladles, and canteens. These were the sort of simple household furnishings that were needed by an agricultural, preindustrial people. A few earthenware animal or human effigies that suggested a more ceremonial side of life had also been found. Most of the Chaco pottery with which I dealt was the end product of a mature craft. It was thin-walled, hard, well-proportioned, and often enriched by sure-handed draftsmanship. Yet I could detect all levels of competence, from that of the all-thumbs bungler to that of the artist. These earthen voices were saying that not all of God's Pueblo Indian children had possessed innate potting skills.

That summer I concluded that since women were assumed to be the engineers, makers, and users of this prehistoric earthenware, women investigators such as I were apt to have a special insight into the domestic fabric of the ancients. I began to feel satisfied that I could have a more meaningful entry into the regional science than merely that which was proffered by default or by what I had erroneously reasoned to be male disinterest.

THE SERIOUS SIDE

During the late 1920s and 1930s, the foundations for the analytical study of prehistoric Puebloan ceramics were being laid by scholars such as Harold Colton, Harold Gladwin, Florence Hawley, Frank Roberts, and Anna Shepard, who formulated the guidelines for nomenclature and description so that all researchers could speak with one voice. Through this ordering of data, the rank and file of regional archaeologists began to see pottery as a useful tool, which, at this preliminary stage of research, they ardently hoped would help to solve one of the most pressing questions concerning the area's prehistory—the time of occupation.

Scientists banked heavily on these earthen artifacts because they were abundant in most of the places where prehistoric farmers had settled. Presumably once the farmers' wives had learned the secrets of the simple, but nevertheless rather miraculous process of converting pliable clay into fire-hardened, inflexible earthenware, they became skilled and prolific at the craft. That was just as well, because as their expertise grew, so did their needs. Faced with having to make the dishes before they could make the meals, they were perhaps the first to moan that a woman's work was never done.

Successful agriculture also drew many more people together into ever larger communities, and life became increasingly complex with a concomitant emphasis on material goods. In order to survive, it was necessary for homes to be filled with dozens of varied receptacles that could be used for a wide gamut of purposes. One can guess that rowdy children, the family dog, an undue shock, or just plain clumsiness had caused the trash dumps beside the villages to be constantly augmented by scattered remains of broken crockery. There they generally lay remarkably undisturbed, in some cases for many centuries.

Although whole pieces of such low-fired pottery were very vulnerable, their sherds did not rot, disintegrate, burn, or attract insects. That durability, combined with an inhospitable environment that did not lure intensive white penetration or settlement until relatively recent times, created an impressive, potentially enlightening resource. Sheer abundance, however, was not enough to account for the importance of pottery to the Southwestern archaeologists at this early stage of the discipline.

The real value that pottery offered to science came from two theoretical dating techniques, made particularly effective by both the nature and depth of many cultural deposits located in the region's recesses, as well as a climatic aridity that forestalled decay of perishables. One concept involved the principle of stratigraphy, wherein the strata of the deposition could be dated relatively according to their positions. This process enabled a chronological dating with the earliest layers being at the bottom, the intermediate layers in-between, and the more recent layers uppermost. This principle had been tested prior to World War I but was first applied on a major scale at Pecos Pueblo during the 1920s.

The other concept was dendrochronology, or the study of overlapping patterns of growth rings in some types of the evergreen trees that were used by the former inhabitants of the Colorado Plateau for construction. It had been less than ten years since a master chart of such overlapping dated tree rings had been completed. Under optimal conditions, this process enabled excavators to ascertain whether life had existed at the sites they were studying at any time from the present almost back to the time of Christ. By applying one or both of these methods at appropriate sites, the recovered pottery could be fit-ted onto a time scaffold with reasonably secure footing. Not all Pueblo ruins yielded datable wood; however, virtually all contained some pottery. Therefore, pottery that was dated at one location could be used to determine the time of Indian habitation if the same kind of wares were found at another site.

The varied geological composition of the sweep of plateaus and deserts that comprised the southwestern United States meant that the raw materials available for making pottery were similarly diverse. The physical variations were matched by a host of manufacturing and stylistic ones. Consequently, over the course of time, identifiable localisms became the norm, even though the basic pottery-making endeavor and the motivations behind it were shared by all the sedentary Southwesterners. In some areas, for example, the iron-bearing clays fired a deep red color, whereas in others, the baked pottery emerged a dirty gray. Some potters learned to add quartz sand to their raw clay to open it up, so that the steam that was driven out by heat had channels of escape and would not crack the vessels. Others turned to crushed rock or potsherds for the same purposes, and these internal substances were in themselves varied. Some potters made pigments for decoration by grinding down mineral oxides and working them into a solution, while their neighbors preferred to use the concentrated juices of certain native plants. Some groups typically decorated their pots with bold, tightly controlled geometrical motifs in a single color; others made use of two colors; and some even preferred a variety of naturalistic elements laid on with abandon. Some used brush as fuel for firing, while others preferred coal, with freely oxidizing atmospheres occasionally purposefully giving way to heavy reduction. These differences, which research was showing to be traceable through time and space, provided concrete evidence of trade relationships that saw pots being distributed from one district to another.

M for Mesoamerica

Awhirlwind romance in the spring of my senior year culminated in a marriage proposal from Bob Lister. He was handsome, self-assured, and fun, and he could easily have won a contest for the best imitation of the Navajo falsetto style of chanting, a talent that enlivened many a dull gathering. Moreover, he was already involved in what I thought to be the most fascinating of vocations. I had not forgotten Dr. Florence's advice. Because Bob promised me a lifetime of love and adventure, I was giddy with happy anticipation. Then came the threat and actuality of war.

The next summer, several days after Bob became a commissioned army officer, we married. Like throngs of others, we shifted for a time from one military post to another, enduring makeshift living arrangements, prolonged separations, and deep anxiety. When Bob's division was shipped overseas, I returned to Los Angeles. The flood of Mexican migrant workers (*braceros*) coming into California made it easy for me to secure a position reading Spanish language mail for the Office of Censorship.

Months of worry over the safety of my man and the inescapable feeling that our youthful years were being stolen from us eroded my schoolgirl dreams. Quixotic fantasies of romping through antiquity in fabled lands were flooded by pent-up emotions. Homemaking, helpmating, and mothering became my top priorities. In the context of my traditional upbringing, this symbolized a return to normalcy.

Following the war and a year in graduate school, my domestic objectives were further solidified as Bob and I entered academic life at the University of Colorado. Bob was the first archaeologist to be hired by the Department of So-

The Lister team

cial Sciences that already included economists, sociologists, political scientists, and a single cultural anthropologist, Omer C. Stewart. While Bob set about working up new study courses, I began to fit comfortably into my new role as a faculty wife. My interest in archaeology did not fade but was redirected.

Soon after our arrival in Boulder, we got the opportunity to become acquainted with Earl Morris when his second wife Lucile invited us to tea. We were understandably thrilled. In ivory tower isolation, Earl Morris was then working out of the lower level of his Boulder hillside home for the Carnegie Institution of Washington. He was a person whose reputation symbolized the excitement and intellectual challenge that had lured so many of our generation into Southwestern archaeology. For over thirty years he had probed sites of all ages across the vast sweep of the Colorado Plateau from the Colorado River to the foot of the Rockies, often being the first to define particular attributes of each. His long-term projects for the American Museum of Natural History led to the establishment of the two national monuments, Aztec Ruins and Canyon de Chelly.

The often embellished retelling of his unparalleled exploits had doubtlessly

*Pioneer archaeologist Earl Morris with special Basketmaker finds made in
Broken Flute Cave, northeastern Arizona, 1930. Hollowed-out tree
limb wrapped with cordage and containing bird feathers*

created a romanticized persona in the popular culture, and my first impression
of this legendary figure was certainly unsettling. Morris was short in stature,
slight in build, soft-spoken, and unassuming. Where was the swashbuckling
action hero exuding raw daring and Scud missile instincts that honed in on
unsuspected treasures? These qualities were not apparent to me during our
first meeting. It now seems all the more ironic that years later, a line drawing
of Morris standing before an ancient houseblock that decorated the cover of
our book, *Earl Morris and Southwestern Archaeology,* was rumored to have inspired the visage of the larger-than-life movie character called Indiana Jones. It
was the hat, of course, worn pulled straight across his forehead, and his steely-
eyed stare that implied this was a man who could and would beat the odds.

First impressions, however, can often be misleading. When Earl gave us a
tour through his spacious workroom full of tables strewn with Basketmaker
artifacts about which I would write years later, I could clearly see the fire in
those eyes. He had not been in the field for more than a decade, but he obvi-

Earl Morris with wooden flute from Broken Flute Cave. The flute more properly should be blown into at the end rather than side. Oscar Tatman, longtime field assistant, in background.

ously relished every artifactual detail; every unyielding slab of stone that had been pried loose; every disheartening empty trench; every unmarked grave with its mute but poignant contributions to the journey onward; and, most especially, every one of the hundreds of pottery vessels he had unearthed or coveted during a lifetime of searching. When he handed us a crudely shaped gray jar and recalled that at the age of three, he had dug it up with his mother's butcher knife, there was no doubting that relish.

During his twilight years when we knew him, Earl Morris gave generously of his time to advise eager students and to share some of the trials and triumphs of a long, distinguished career with public audiences. The talks were presented matter-of-factly, as though all of the gray-haired armchair enthusiasts and academicians whose tedious days were spent before microscopes or behind lecterns had participated in the same experiences. He could scarcely fathom that there actually might be persons who had not bounced for six days across an uncharted wilderness in a mule-drawn wagon to shovel into a heap of collapsed masonry that once had been an Indian home; who had not dug by lantern light to retrieve a fragmentary aboriginal ladder; who had not passed snowbound winter days reassembling shattered pots shaped by anonymous prehistoric hands to keep their households functioning; or who had not lifted exquisitely woven doghair sashes from a bark-lined cist in a dusty cave out in the middle of Navajo nowhere. Earl acted like it was all in a day's work, but one suspected that inwardly, he had never ceased to marvel at the blessed providence that had afforded him such pleasure.

In a final conversation with Al Lancaster, another key supporting actor in the unfolding drama of regional studies, I listened as he reflected upon Bob's reaction to Earl's sudden death in 1956, news of which reached us during breakfast at the university's Mesa Verde field school. With tears streaming down his cheeks, Bob had quietly mourned the loss of a man who had quickly become his friend and role model and at the same time recognized the inevitable end of an era that had given both flavor and fact to the pursuit of knowledge.

Our circle of friends also expanded to include a few women who were trying to make it in the man's world of archaeology. I saw that, knowingly or not, in order to counter the bias weighted against them, they had been forced to make sacrifices in their personal lives that I was not prepared to make. Although later I was to learn that they could not be so easily classified, in my shallow experience I mentally put them into three categories.

Group A was the "anything you can do, I can do better" school. Primarily that meant appearing as masculine as possible in their dress and grooming, defiantly hanging tough under field conditions that would have devastated most of the so-called weaker sex, and cultivating aggressive, roustabout behavior and vocabulary. All of this was window dressing totally unrelated to their scientific accomplishments. Group B was composed of the neutral, mousey creatures who retreated into their working realms without concern for the real world, much less for the men who dominated it. Group C was comprised of those women whose femininity had not been compromised and who resented but quietly accepted male professional prejudice while still enjoying male social companionship. In the remote possibility that I would ever have the opportunity of joining those ranks, I thought I most likely would fit into Group C's company.

My chance to test the waters came in the summer of 1952. The first six weeks was a breaking-in period of coping with life in the field with a five-year-old son Frank and a second son Gary, who had just turned two. Bob teamed up with Marie Wormington of the Denver Museum of Natural History to excavate some middens in the lee of a cliff located at the base of the Uncompahgre Plateau in western Colorado.

I had first seen Marie Wormington at the Fourth Chaco Anthropological Conference (later named the Seventh Pecos Conference) in 1940, when several of us who were students were permitted to stay after the field school had ended in order to attend what Brand turned into a Mexican extravaganza to commemorate the 400th anniversary of Francisco Vásquez de Coronado's fateful *entrada* into New Mexico. Actually my most vivid memory there was of Daniel Rubín de la Borbolla, of the Instituto Politécnico Nacional, who with his sleek Latin handsomeness and dashing ascot tie worn with great elan, was the meeting's answer to Rudolph Valentino. As for Marie, she struck me as a Group C female archaeologist—trim, attractive, poised, and worldly. I remember thinking, "this is it!"

When Marie and I became acquainted after our move to Boulder, I found that she confirmed my first impressions. She liked good clothes, a refined home, and creative cooking. I did think it quaintly unconventional that she retained her maiden name after marriage. Now this sign of independence is commonplace, but Marie was the first woman I ever knew to do so. I was undecided whether she kept her name because she had begun her career before marriage or because she was determined to retain her own identity. Her husband, Pete Volk, was a large robust man who looked like a prizefighter because he had broken his nose while playing college football. Around Marie, however, he was gentle as a pussy cat. He hung in the background during the many parties they gave for her associates, always ready to light Marie's next cigarette or fetch her next drink.

As successful as Marie appeared to be, however, she had not totally escaped gender bias. She began her work at the Denver Museum for a pittance that would have been unacceptable to her male colleagues. As a graduate student at Radcliffe College, she had been one of the several women who were permitted to attend lectures at Harvard as long as they sat in the hall and listened through an open doorway. There in the male bastion of Peabody Museum, she had even been forced to endure disgruntled remarks about the scent of her perfume (of all things!). Marie liked to joke about these incidents, but she al-

Archaeologists' sons at work in Chaco Canyon field station,
1952. Gary, age 2, at left; Frank, age 5, at right

ways did so with an air of resignation. I could not help but wonder, however, if she had chosen to specialize and earn an international reputation in what were then the traditional male fields of Paleo-Indian prehistory and lithic technology out of some sense of defiance.

Something else I learned about Marie was that although she was a fastidious housekeeper, her field camps were disorderly and dirty. She was not alone among archaeologists in quickly sloughing off the niceties of conventional living once she had reached a dig site. That summer of 1952 an abandoned farmhouse, musty with pack rat droppings and strips of wallpaper hanging limp from the soiled walls, had been mucked out with the help of several of Pete's football buddies to provide crude bunk facilities for the crew. We, however, chose to pitch our family tent in the isolation of an adjoining sagebrush flat.

It was by no means my first experience at roughing it. Several entire summers and innumerable weekends during my childhood had been spent in the mountains of Colorado and on the California deserts where my father attempted to make a living at hardrock mining. But that was before I had an inkling of

The dry road to Chihuahua, Mexico, mountain archaeological sites

how small a tent could be with two active boys. In our Colorado camp, they soon began spending their days happily chasing lizards and driving toy trucks and tractors through the mounded dirt under the tent fly. For maternal reasons, I increasingly looked forward to our weekly excursions to the Laundromat and to the swimming pool in the nearest town.

Already dirtied and worn, in mid-July we broke camp, repacked, and departed for a second summer project. Together with five students, our young family headed for the mountains that form a formidable wall between the northern Mexican states of Chihuahua and Sonora. Aided by a modest research grant, Bob intended to launch a three-season exploration of some caves that were worn into cliffs and known to contain evidence of former human occupation. We crossed the international border at El Paso and drove south by convoy on the newly completed Central Pan American Highway to the point where a rough track veered off toward the west. Its two ruts cut upward over rocky ridges and downward across successive wide, treeless, alkali-frosted *playas,* eventually terminating in Nuevo Casas Grandes. It was one hundred miles of emptiness broken only by an occasional stock tank or windmill, and a few straggling cows of mixed breeding who were seeking the spotty shade of mesquite clumps. The route took five hours to negotiate through clouds of choking dust that were kicked up by a hot desert wind.

Nuevo Casas Grandes, the regional commercial center, was a line of basic ugly buildings that had been thrown up along both sides of the railroad tracks that linked the region to the state capital several hundred miles to the south. The original town of Casas Grandes, located a few miles farther west, remained a quiet rural village of squat adobe houses built around a leafy plaza, its residents seemingly unconcerned about the doubtful noisy progress of their sister community. We camped peacefully nearby for the night.

The next morning we pushed on toward the mountains that were becoming more prominent on the western horizon. Crossing gravelly, barren plateaus, the road abruptly turned downward into a narrow shallow valley shaded coolly by fruit orchards. The dramatic contrast between the natural physical environments both beyond and within this haven was matched only by a man-made one—a tiny country hamlet of solid red brick houses with tow-headed, blue-eyed youngsters playing in the yards, well-tended kitchen gardens, and dirt lanes lined by ditches running full of irrigation water. With good reason, it all had the appearance of Utah. We discovered that this was a community of transplanted American Mormons who were the descendants of families who had fled across the border during the 1870s because of recently enacted U.S. laws prohibiting the practice of polygamy.

Assuring us that the lumber road leading back into the mountains to the area of our immediate destination, Cave Valley, was impassable for our automobiles, two of the local men volunteered to take us there in a high-clearance weapons carrier they had recently acquired as army surplus. We dumped our tents, our digging gear, and ourselves onto the vehicle's open back for a gut-wrenching afternoon career into the wilderness. Finally arriving at the edge of a constricted valley along the Rio Piedras Verdes, one of the small waterways that flow through the eastern slopes of the Sierra Madre Occidental, our new Mormon friends unloaded us and promised to return in three weeks. Although there appeared to be some contemporary habitation in the valley, we would essentially have no ready contact with the outside world. Cut off as we were going to be, we did not consider the possible problems that might have ensued in this isolation if someone in our party had required emergency medical help. Youth and inexperience do in fact cultivate derring-do.

As it turned out, we camped along the main crossing of the valley bottom that connected the half-dozen desolate rancherías, which could be spotted

Off to Cave Valley. Lister boys and father in center background; mother in center row

Dealing with local Cave Valley merchants

Olla Cave granary, Cave Valley, Chihuahua

through the opening below the cliffs. Once our presence was discovered, the amount of traffic back and forth along that trail far surpassed the presumed normal occupation levels. Obviously our arrival was the most interesting event to have broken the monotony of life in Cave Valley for a very long time. Soon dirty, ragged children in twos and threes appeared at the edge of the camp on the pretext of selling us stacks of tortillas tied up in soiled napkins or an egg or two still warm from the hens' nests. Actually they were intent on taking in all the uncommon novelty of strangers among their midst. Since I had become camp cook, it became my task to deal with these native merchants.

A daily routine was established that included morning explorations into the trash deposits and cellular structures that were located in five protective openings weathered midway up a cliff face about a mile away. Afternoons were spent in camp working with notes and recovered artifacts. As I had time, I again took up washing and examining pottery fragments. They were then put into cloth ore sample bags and stacked beside our tent to be taken back to the university for a later, more detailed analysis.

We had been in Cave Valley for a week, when one day as I was preparing the noon meal, I saw four or five men ride up on horses and dismount just beyond the camp clearing. They silently squatted on their haunches by the trail and stared at me. Alone except for Gary and unnerved by what seemed to be strange behavior on their part, I busied myself at my task. From what I could see, the men were all clothed in mismatched country garb and were unshaven. There was no doubt in my mind that they were all bandits. After all, this was former Pancho Villa country. With forced casualness, I stepped into our tent, rapidly hid my diamond rings in my tennis shoes, stuffed my wallet into a sleeping bag, and bravely emerged to face the dangers of confrontation. The men remained as they were—still at a distance, still silent, still staring. It was a Mexican stand-off. After what seemed like an eternity, I saw with considerable relief that Bob, Frank, and the students were coming down the trail. The strangers stood up, waylaid Bob, and engaged him in an intent conversation while the others came on into camp. In a few minutes Bob followed, unsmiling. He told us that he would have to go with the men for a while. Then he returned to the group of visitors, mounted a horse·behind one of their saddles, and rode off. I felt just like a heroine in a Grade B movie, with my love riding off to his final reward at the hands of a posse.

It was late afternoon before the boys spotted their dad wearily trudging down the path toward camp. We all rushed out to learn what had prompted those mysterious events at noon. Bob explained that the local posse had set itself up as a watchdog committee and had stopped him requesting to see our digging permit. Such authorization is legally mandatory, because in Mexico all antiquities belong to the federal government regardless of whether they are found on public or on private land. Although the cave sites were not maintained monuments with a caretaker, officials had impressed upon the peasants the responsibility of protecting them. In principle, we applauded this conscientious diligence, for there were already signs of vandalism in the cliff dwellings despite their inaccessibility. In actuality, however, the action of the valley men was embarrassing to us, because by the time we reached our destination, we realized that we had inadvertently left our government permit on a park bench in Albuquerque as we waited there for a doctor to treat Frank's eye following a minor mishap on the way south. After realizing our mistake, we had wired Mexico City for a copy of the papers, but we had little hope of receiving it and had therefore decided to bluff our way through. After all, in our own minds our expedition's purpose was legitimate, and it had been approved. If worst came to worst, we reasoned that we could clear ourselves by writing a few telegrams to colleagues at the capital. Now, however, we had unfortunately been caught like common criminals.

The men had taken Bob to a small schoolhouse where they sat around a table to interrogate him. Always polite and respectful in the way that humble country folk are when they are somewhat awed by persons they judge to be of a higher social standing, they were nevertheless correctly forceful in their objections to our lack of official papers. They probably could not have read them but they would have been reassured by a battery of impressive seals and stamps. Bob had struggled to explain himself and his work as he had never done before. In desperation he drew upon dormant Spanish vocabulary from the inner recesses of his mind. Slowly it became apparent that although ruin despoliation had been a consideration, the real reason for the inquest was that his tribunal thought we had motives other than merely archaeological ones. The ore sacks lying by our camp and visible from the trail outwardly seemed to be suspicious indications of enrichment. With hindsight, we realized that we had been stupid not to anticipate the false impression these sacks might give, since lost treasure is a deeply embedded part of Southwestern folklore on both sides of the international border. As the afternoon wore on, Bob felt he had won over his jury one-by-one with his descriptions of his program and of his genuine interest in learning about and protecting the local antiquities. It was merely an unfortunate incident, he explained, that had prevented him from having all of the required documents within his possession. They were surely in the Nuevo Casas Grandes post office. ¡Que lastima!

After about four hours, the group had slowly relaxed and decided that Bob could leave to continue his work. One man ended the ordeal by telling Bob that he spoke poor Spanish, but lots of it! Then the men had stomped outside, mounted their noble steeds, and trotted off, leaving Bob to walk the five miles back down the valley to our camp. Dejected but relieved, he was a free man. And, as he explained, the code of this country did not allow men to come into a home or a camp where a woman was visibly alone. That was why I had not been approached. Thank God for medieval chivalry, which was still alive in the breasts of Spain's offspring, however removed they might be!

The next day exactly the same sequence of events began to unfold. At approximately the time that the crew was due back in camp, the identical contingent of local men arrived, dismounted, sat by the trail, and watched. When Bob came along, they stopped him. What now? A few minutes later Bob came on to the tent. Smiling, he handed me four small earthenware pots. After yesterday's conversations, it seemed that the men, feeling guilty, had decided that the pottery they had illegally removed from the ruins themselves should be placed in professional hands. Bob had indeed won them over.

As promised the Mormons returned, and we transferred camp to an apple orchard upriver from the village of Colonia Juárez. Our plan was to test a nearby open site to determine if its occupation had been the same type as that in the mountains. Before we left Cave Valley, nighttime electrical storms had ricocheted up and down the escarpments in an awesome display. Now the seasonal rains began in earnest, turning the ruin and our camp into mud sloughs. The tents leaked, our clothes and supplies were drenched, the boys were walking mudpies, and crew morale steadily declined. Again we moved on. This time we went to the only hotel in Nuevo Casas Grandes.

As one downpour followed another, we became marooned, since the three dirt roads leading out to pavement a hundred miles in any direction lay under growing lagoons. No traffic was moving at all, and the train by which we had considered shipping our cars, our equipment, our artifacts, and ourselves to civilization was not due for a week. We therefore reluctantly settled in.

There were few diversions to help us pass the time. Even in good weather, it took us only a few minutes to explore the whole town. The sole movie house had only one record on its loud speaker that blared day and night, and it had only one film on the screen. The hotel lobby contained a few pieces of dusty, broken-down furniture and a few months-old tabloids. The bars were dirty and disgusting. There was nothing else. We all prayed for escape.

Realizing that the only thing that was about to dry up was our research money, the students fended for themselves during the long days. We then all met for a communal evening meal at what passed for the town's best restaurant, situated across the tracks from the hotel. The first night as we were waiting for our food to arrive, a large brown woman wearing a greasy apron cinched about her middle loudly burst through the kitchen door viciously banging a broom at a fleeing mouse. With several well-placed blows, she flattened her victim. Then she nonchalantly walked back to her stove, leaving the rodent squirming where he had fallen. As we sat down at our table the next night, I saw that the dead mouse still lay there undisturbed. On the third night, with the mouse still interred in the same place, I could no longer eat.

Exercising his prerogatives as director of this waterlogged expedition, Bob had taken the only remaining hotel room with bath for his family. The students somehow had to make their ways to an outdoor privy in the patio by walking through a watery swamp of drifted trash and chicken droppings. Although we shared our bathroom with an adjoining room, I took advantage of having it at our disposal and tried to wash some of the mud out of the boys' clothes. The garments were then draped over the sparse room furnishings but they did not dry.

A Mennonite family of four from a sizable colony to the south of Casas Grandes lived in the neighboring room, which shared the bathroom with ours. A small boy and girl with forlorn faces and dressed in a bib overall and long, dark Mother Hubbard dress were carbon copies of their parents. Through the thin walls we could hear them conversing in German. It was immediately evident that this family was not familiar with the workings of flush plumbing. That was even more revolting than the restaurant mouse had been. I sat on the edge of the sagging bed, stared through a fringe of wet socks and jockey shorts at the rain beating incessantly on the dirt yard below, and pondered upon the illusiveness of the glamour of archaeology.

Days dragged by until at last, a stroke of good luck materialized for us. A restless truck driver let it be known that he was going to make an attempt to reach the Central Highway. Bob rushed over to strike a deal with him to let our convoy follow. The plan was that if we got stuck, he would stand by to pull us out. Just as added insurance, we would take his son with us in our station wagon.

The road was as bad as had been rumored. Great bodies of brown water shimmered where weeks before there had been ankle-deep dust or cement-like flats. At the first *playa* where the road dipped into a depression, the truck stalled and became hopelessly mired in a field of oozing mud. On drier ground, we all pulled around him, waved, and slowly continued on our way up over rises and down again into soaked sinks. Often proceeding under what would have been fender-deep water had our cars been so equipped, we hoped that our motors would not drown out, since that would have halted our procession for good. It was getting dark when the thin black line of the highway blessedly

The wet road out

loomed before us. We pulled up to wait for our erstwhile rescuer. Not knowing we were in a spot notorious for tarantulas and totally relieved to be at the end of a severe trial, we stretched out on the warm, wonderfully hard road to watch the stars begin to flicker between the clouds. Hours later the roar of an ill-tuned motor announced the arrival of the larger vehicle. The truck driver wearily reported that he had been stuck three times and had been forced to dig himself out.

Having at last returned our hostage to his parent, our small party quickly sped southward, arriving at the outskirts of Chihuahua City about two in the morning. There we gleefully found a new motel with clean, dry accommodations for all. Wearily we tumbled into our rooms, not even minding that the advertized hot water was in the toilet and not in the lavatory.

THE SERIOUS SIDE

It was not some harebrained search for adventure that had brought us to this remote sierra. The region was considered to be an extension of the Greater Southwest, both culturally as well as geographically. Its known antiquities differed from anything that could be found deeper inside Mexico. Conventional wisdom prior to the 1950s hypothesized that the mountain caves had provided refuge for Pueblo-like Indians who, for some unknown reasons, had deserted the plains to the east. Bob wanted to ascertain the correctness of this idea. Within some of the mountain overhangs, the simple architecture of cube-like adobe and stone rooms, roofed with parallel poles and mud, seemed to represent an architectural technique that was inferior to the one in the most notable plains town, a large unexcavated site situated on a low, sandy escarpment above the Rio Casas Grandes.

As an assortment of tattered perishables, a few stone objects, several human burials, and mounds of potsherds began to grow, it became increasingly evident that the traditional theory of this area's cultural history was incorrect. The pottery with which I worked exhibited a particularly conflicting set of circumstances. Unexpectedly there was very little of the finely made black, red, and tan polychrome pottery that had been characteristic of the settlements on the plains and dated generally from the eleventh and twelfth centuries. Instead, the most usual sherds were of a coarse plain brownware that had been made into very simple utilitarian forms. Rarely there were broadly applied red decorations. The combined data suggested not only an occasional occupation distinctive from the better-known one along the foothills, but also an earlier one. We believed it to be the southernmost extension of the Mogollon culture, which had just become recognized to the north along the New Mexico–Arizona border.

A second objective of our work in the northwestern Mexican mountains was to determine if some identifiable links could be found between the cultures of central Mexico and those of the Southwest. Here in northern Mexico was what was commonly referred to as The Gap, an areal as well as a cultural void. Two elements were thought to be possible links that reflected a northward ideological diffusionary trajectory from Mexico to the Southwest at different times. One was the pottery-making technology that was exemplified by the cave finds. The other was the discovery of a primitive type of corn that had been recovered at depths far below the cave structures and indicated an early experimentation with horticulture. Unfortunately, at that time neither kind of evidence was dated.

During the next few years Bob returned to Chihuahua for several seasons to continue his mountain research. Together during a number of spring breaks, our family visited old *haciendas,* mining camps, missions, and Tarahumaran

Departing from Chihuahua mountain rancheria for an archaeological survey

villages; and we even rode on the Chihuahua al Pacífico railroad a month after it had been completed following ninety-odd years of construction. Some time after our Cave Valley trip, the road to Casas Grandes was paved, and the archaeological site there was excavated by two of our old friends, Charlie Di Peso and Arnie Withers. They confirmed the thesis that exotic central Mexican influence had continued into the post-Mogollon eras. The excavations demonstrated that in its prime, Casas Grandes had probably been instrumental in the transmission of Mexican goods and ideas to Chaco Canyon during the eleventh and twelfth centuries.

In the mid-1960s the results of these various studies were published in our survey book, *Chihuahua, Storehouse of Storms,* which dealt with the history of that area from prehistoric times to the present. Our book emphasized the historical interactions between this northern section of Mexico and the southwestern part of the United States. After experiencing a shared prehistoric culture on several levels, other parts of that common background mosaic included the presence of the *conquistadores* who passed through Chihuahua on their way to establish Spain's northernmost colony of New Mexico; the trail down the central plateau linking that province to Mexico City; the fearsome Comanches and Apaches sweeping out of the north to terrorize Chihuahuan whites; the American occupation during the mid-nineteenth century; the arrival of the Utah Mormons; and Pancho Villa's raid into Columbus, New Mexico, along with General Pershing's retaliatory pursuit.

Sixteen years later after some of the information had become outdated, Chihuahua's governor, or someone on his staff, discovered our book and declared it to be the state's "official" history. This was just another of the many regional incongruities, since we happened to be neither residents nor Mexicans. Our book was subsequently translated into Spanish, and special, leather-bound copies were presented to the President of the Republic and to all of the Mexican state governors, while cheaper editions went on sale to the public. We and the director of the University of New Mexico Press, who published our book, were invited to be the honored guests at a special *fiesta*. For two days there were excursions, presentations of plaques and scrolls, flowery speeches at the city hall and state capitol, toasts to international good will and to the *gringo* historians, and many *abrazos*. If only the vigilantes of Cave Valley could have seen us then!

Two years following our initial Chihuahuan experience, we again went to central Mexico for the 1953–1954 academic year, when Bob received a Ford Foundation Fellowship to review Mexican archaeology. His doctoral dissertation at Harvard had dealt with one aspect of western Mexican prehistory, and we had spent six months after his release from the Infantry visiting Mexican digs, museums, and monuments from border to border. So much research was under way at the time, however, that an update was essential for his teaching and investigative goals. We went to Mexico City, rented a one-bedroom apartment with cot space for the boys—that being the extent of our available funds—and converted the grant money into Mexican currency in a local bank account. Within a week, the peso had been devaluated, and the next day the price of everything rose. This effectively cut at least one month off of our intended stay.

Academically, the winter was a success. Bob was given access to unpublished excavation notes, and I had time to explore the city and review the museum pottery collections. We also became intimately familiar with the prehistory of Mexico's diverse districts and met a group of concerned scientists working on associated problems. This group included people such as Ignacio Marquina, Eduardo Noguera, the suave Rubín de la Borbolla, Paul Kirckhoff, and Isabel Kelly, whom we had seen at Brand's conference in Chaco before the war.

A visitor from home that winter was Bertha Dutton, a woman who had graduated from the University of New Mexico during Bob's time there. Edgar Lee Hewett, for whom she had worked as secretary while in school, had made her Curator of Ethnology at the Museum of New Mexico, and we had met occasionally at meetings and at social gatherings. Now while she was on a trip to Mexico to gather background information for her doctoral dissertation, we convoyed around the countryside inspecting many archaeological zones, she in the Model A sedan she drove until it became a museum piece.

In part, Bert belonged to my Group A female prehistorians. Growing up on a farm in the Midwest, she looked as if she had never left it. She was short, stocky, and unless absolutely necessary, seldom out of jeans that frequently had a bandanna hanging from a back pocket. She wore no makeup, and her hair was cut in a severe mannish bob that was slicked down with glistening pomade. As the years went by, I was amused to realize that a bit of vanity caused her to use tint to hide the gray. Unpolished but friendly and eager to have social as well as professional recognition, I felt that in private, she was a lonely woman. She never married, and during the last several decades of her life, she shared her home with a female companion.

Since the Chihuahuan trip with our children had been accomplished without too much strain, I foolhardily viewed our next Mexican venture as a lark. It was not quite so. We enrolled both boys, ages three and six, in one of the city's bilingual schools. This turned out to be an exasperating learning experience for us all. First the boys unsuccessfully rebelled daily at having to wear uniforms. As far as they were concerned, T-shirts and jeans were what a kid ought to wear. Then a major crisis ensued most afternoons when I tried to augment Frank's first grade English reading, writing, and spelling skills, which had been inadequately handled by a Mexican teacher who did not know the language. At an end-of-term awards program the school staff, obviously at a loss to know how to include these two little outsiders, gave each of the boys a medal to pin on their chests for proficiency in English! I thought I deserved at least some of the credit.

Health problems also left me questioning the wisdom of ever leaving home with my brood until they graduated from high school, despite the allure of archaeological attractions. Although I carefully monitored the family's food and drink, well-meaning strangers frequently plied my appealing blond youngsters with goodies that their systems could not tolerate. Two children vomiting simultaneously during the middle of the night was not a comforting sight. Then in the fall, Frank developed an undiagnosed recurrent fever, and he subsequently broke his arm falling off his bike. Of course, that happened during another of a long string of holidays, but fortunately a doctor could be found. After this incident, both boys got chicken pox. Then Bob had chicken pox. In the spring Frank's fever persistently continued periodically. He broke the same arm a second time in a different place. Finally, both boys contracted the mumps. On the day we began our long drive back to Colorado, Bob also came down with the mumps. For two days we hibernated in a motel in Aguascalientes while he recovered.

Then we drove on to Durango where we had an appointment with Aggie Howard, an expatriated Texas woman interested in the prehistory of the Durango area. During the winter she had taken Bob on a week-long horseback ride through the rugged mountains that separate the central plateau from the coastal plains of Sinaloa to show him some sites she had found, hoping to interest him in their investigation. They agreed to collaborate on an article, but I was uncertain of our welcome at this particular time since Aggie had six children. Fortunately several were away from home, and the others had already had the mumps. We made plans to return for some testing as soon as it was feasible. This, however, would not occur until the spring of 1958.

Our base of operations for the Durango work was to be the Howard ranch, half a day's distance into the *sierra* west of the capital city. A friend flew Aggie and me there in the comfort of his private plane. Mac Howard and several of his sons trucked Bob and the boys in, slowly proceeding over a tortuous track. En route they passed a local point of interest—a movie set consisting of an abandoned *hacienda* complex and *peon* quarters, where a number of Hollywood film makers had chosen to make westerns because of the area's smog-free blue skies. Yul Brynner, Steve McQueen, and Robert Mitchum became Durango household names, almost but not quite on a par with Cantinflas and Manolete. In his later years, Mac gave up his lifelong occupation of punching cows to retire to the easier, more lucrative business of renting props to these productions.

The ranch headquarters was a fascinating, stark reminder of the Old West. A cluster of block-shaped adobe structures sat in a cup of land that was surrounded by dry rocky hills and dotted with scrubby brush, wild oregano, and a few multi-armed towering *pitaya* cacti. No efforts had been wasted on beautifying the house or the surrounding yard, since this was an old-fashioned outfit that focused entirely on working range cattle. The boys were entranced at their first contact with real live cowboys going about their daily tasks and with the occasional colorful Huichol Indian wandering through. They were eager to be a part of the activities of the younger Howards, and they tried to prove themselves by doing chores to which they had never before been exposed. Since Gary, then about eight and small for his age, was the youngest of the lot, he felt he had to outwork and outrun the other boys. When he downed a whole can of torrid serrano chilies topped by sardines on a dare, however, it really seemed that *machismo* had gotten out-of-hand.

Aside from the current price of beef on the hoof, our main topic of conversation at mealtimes was the local terror—deadly scorpions that infested the vicinity. Their stings could bring quick convulsions and death within twenty-four hours. Maybe the talk was mainly for the benefit of us greenhorns, but I was nevertheless nervous. Little boys are known for leaping before looking, and I have been a human magnet for all kinds of biting insects my whole life. Since the tack room where we slept seemed an ideal scorpion breeding ground, we therefore made it our practice to carefully scan our bedrolls with a flashlight each night to make certain that we had no unwelcome insect visitors, and to shake out our clothes each morning before we got dressed. Somehow we eventually left Durango unscathed.

Although Mac made it plain that he thought work such as ours was damned foolishness, he nevertheless provided us with three horses and a laborer as an indulgence to his wife. Frank, then eleven, had his own mount. Gary had to be content with riding behind Bob's saddle. Once when he was inattentive during a climb up a steep slope, he slid backward right off the

Ranch headquarters, Durango, Mexico

horse's rump. For both boys such adventures were exhilarating, known to them previously only in books or movies. In their new Mexican straw hats and sitting atop their horses, I thought they lived up to their youthful nicknames of Pancho and Garito.

The site was about an hour-and-a-half ride from the ranch on a trail that wound up vertical inclines, edged out over exposed slick rock where footing was precarious, eased along narrow precipices that abruptly dropped off into rocky gullies, and eventually ascended a round promontory called Cerro Bollo, or Hill of the Bulge. The old settlement on its crest had consisted of a string of rooms, but rough stone outlines were all that now remained. It must have once been a defensive lookout with a breathtaking view overlooking an accordion-folded expanse of barren, jagged slopes descending into a deep narrow river valley where a stand of cottonwoods and a few hardy residents struggled for life. Even though the valley was miles away, a braying burro clearly could be heard in the still, clear air.

After laying a proper grid, Bob and his helper commenced digging out the compacted fill in several rooms. The boys and I stationed ourselves at the pile of spoil dirt to retrieve any artifacts. In the early afternoon, we paused to partake of the lunch sent by the ranch cook—a worn pillow case containing the customary rations of the mountains. It was an indigestible concoction of cornmeal balls rolled around a bit of chili-flavored meat braised in a chili sauce. They were aptly called *gorditas,* or little fat ones. I opted instead for the hard-skinned oranges that had been trucked up from the tropical coast.

The ancient structure proved to have been erected on bedrock. After it was abandoned, only a shallow drift of windborne dirt had accumulated. There were few artifacts other than potsherds, but they were what initially caught Bob's attention, since at the time both he and J. Charles Kelley, a Southwestern colleague teaching at Southern Illinois University, were defining a regional culture known as Chalchihuites, after a large ruin having the same name.

THE SERIOUS SIDE

The typical Chalchihuites pottery designs of small life forms such as lizards, snakes, and birds resembled those favored by the Hohokam people who had once lived in the Salt, Gila, and Santa Cruz river valleys, where Phoenix and Tucson now sprawl. There were other material goods found in the Hohokam remains that were also alien to the known aboriginal Southwest, and they were presumed to be of Mexican origin. Added to the pottery, these traits suggested that a route of diffusion led from the mountain masses that separated the modern states of Durango and Sinaloa—part of the same massif of the Sierra Madre Occidental farther north—and may have spread up the western coast littoral to the Arizona deserts. Alternatively, however, the Chalchihuites and the Hohokam potteries may have developed from a common source. In either case, the Mexican connections to the Southwest, such as early corn agriculture and pottery-making, which Bob had discovered in Chihuahua, were being attacked on another front.

Of immediate interest to students of pottery like me was the realization that there were probably two distinct streams of ceramic diffusion flowing at more or less the same time from central Mexico into the Southwest. One stream moved northward as part of the Hohokam cultural package. It remained committed to a basically red-and-tan palette derived from iron-bearing clays and from a firing technique that produced an oxidizing atmosphere. As the Hohokam culture matured in the Arizona deserts, this advancement was reflected both in the wide range of vessel forms and in the decorations adorning them. In contrast, the Mogollon people seemed to have learned of pottery-making as an idea passed on to them by others. Since their cultural growth beyond an Archaic hunting and gathering subsistence had been only modest, Mogollon pottery-making remained a craft executed only on a rudimentary level that yielded low-fired, drab brown ceramics of elementary shapes. The most outstanding contribution of the Mogollon potters prior to A.D. 1000 was their service as transmitters of ceramic knowledge to their northern neighbors, the ancestral Pueblos, who over the course of a millennium-and-a-half converted domestic necessities into works of art.

Two weeks of excavation work at Cerro Bollo exhausted that site's possibilities. Bob therefore decided to take his data and artifacts, together with the other information and photographs that had been supplied by Aggie, south to Guadalajara. There in some comfort, we could work on our report and get the boys back into school. Before leaving the ranch, however, he wanted to see the well-known but remote site of Cueva Pitaya.

Getting to Cueva Pitaya meant a strenuous four-hour ride each way, but by then we felt that we had become fairly well-broken-in to the saddle. Mac obligingly gave us horses and two wranglers. They added interest to our ride, dressed as they were in their loose cotton shirts and pants, with bright bandannas tied around their throats, thick *huaraches* soled with slabs cut from old rubber tires on their feet, and sweat-stained straw hats shading their eyes. In their belts they wore wickedly sharp machetes to cut away obstructing thorny growth if the necessity arose.

After an uneventful ride and the usual *gordita* and orange lunch, we set out to explore the cave. Cueva Pitaya was a yawning, arched opening located near the talus that poured from a cliff where human beings had found shelter within its protection. This was evidenced by simple storage cists, by spots where camps had been, and by rocks that had been blackened from the smoke of both ancient and modern fires. A relatively deep earthen fill containing traces of man's refuse exuded the mustiness of centuries. At one side a secondary small opening in the rocks suggested that another possible place had also been available for human use. Frank and Gary set out to explore it.

As an archaeological mother, I vowed early on not to turn these inquisitive youths into fearful ninnies by transferring my own innate caution to them. Nor did I intend to unnecessarily curb the fun or intellectual growth our particular way of life afforded them. Therefore, on this occasion I stilled my maternal instincts and let them go. On their hands and knees in the soft dirt, the boys

Cueva Pitaya, Durango, where humans have sought shelter for centuries

worked their way along a confined natural shaft back into the cliff as the passageway steadily became darker and smellier. After crawling some yards, the explorers reached a small cavern. Their efforts were rewarded by finding some discarded arrow shafts and a bit of woven fiber that once might have been part of a worn sandal. Then the roving beam from their flashlight revealed a cluster of bats clinging upside-down to the cave ceiling. Surely bats must be among the Lord's ugliest creatures, and these were the first of their species that the boys had ever viewed. As several of the disturbed flying mammals swished down over them, the children turned tail and rushed pell-mell out into the sunlight, thoroughly frightened, but unharmed.

The day drew to an end as we roughly smoothed out a sleeping spot on the flat ground away from the cave opening, spread our saddle blankets as a base for our sleeping bags, and sat down to eat a cold snack. Suddenly, as if someone had closed the drapes, it became a black, moonless night. We crawled into our beds, the two boys lying prone between their two tired parents. Off in the distance we could hear the hobbled horses thrashing about through the dry brush, and the muted voices of the wranglers told us that they had made their own camp farther on.

As we lay watching the blanket of stars blossom overhead, it crossed my mind that in this craggy land that was far removed from civilization, we were very much at the mercy of these strangers. Intentionally or not, they looked quite fierce with their dark complexions and their machetes worn with such casual bravado. These mountains, which today are reported to be the pivotal territory of ruthless drug operations, were even then notorious for the lawlessness of their inhabitants. Mac had told us many hair-raising accounts of easy murder or banditry. Even after living there for fifteen years, he always still warily kept a loaded gun close at hand, and saw to it that the windows of his house were above head height and that his children never went unattended. My fatigue was so great that even these worrisome thoughts could not keep me awake.

Sometime during the middle of the night, I suddenly awoke to hear Frank whimpering and moving about. As mothers learn to do in their sleep, I put my hand on his forehead. He was shaking uncontrollably, not from a chill, but from fright. He whispered that he had heard a branch snap near our beds. In the darkness nothing was visible, and I mustered enough courage to assure him that it had just been a prowling animal. He would not be comforted and continued to tremble. The poor child was terrorized by an overdose of unfamiliar environments, by his episodes with the bats and the scorpions, and perhaps by the same vague uneasiness that I also felt. We therefore cuddled close together for the remainder of a long sleepless night.

Daylight was reassuring. While the wranglers readied the horses, we nibbled at a few dry *pan dulces* and oranges. Eager to leave what we now regarded as an evil place, we mounted as soon as possible to return to the security of the ranch. Out on the trail as we plodded mile after mile in single file, the Mexican lead rider in front of me suddenly reined up, jumped off his horse, and whipped out his dreaded machete. Involuntarily I gasped. This was it. The man then stepped off the trail, leaned over, and deftly sliced his weapon through the air. With a broad grin, he turned and presented me with the most exquisite waxy cactus flower I had ever seen! Words could not express the chagrin I felt at my earlier suspicions of him. As a dedicated part of an anthropological team, I hoped that this incident would teach us all a little lesson about mistrusting others simply because their appearance, language, and ways differed from our own, but as a strained, very tired mother, I doubted that it would.

Once we reached Guadalajara, we realized that because Holy Week was imminent, there would be no school. We therefore hastily decided to fly south to the classic Mayan site of Palenque, where a few years earlier, the first tomb inside a New World pyramid had been discovered. Because the boys had never before flown, we went to great pains to prepare them for a special treat. Within half an hour after take-off, however, Frank was green and Gary was losing his breakfast. We had not realized that the abrupt plunge from the lofty Mexican plateau to the Caribbean coast would cause this to be an especially turbulent flight. Once at Villahermosa, the jumping-off point for Palenque, my first errand was to rush to a pharmacy where I purchased two Dramamine tablets for the return flight. Although we were going back to Mexico City by a different route, I was taking no chances.

In those days there were no means of public transportation into the village near the archaeological zone of Palenque. Therefore, we went to the small Villahermosa airport and chartered a four-seater plane to take us the rest of the way. Bob sat beside the pilot, while the rest of us squeezed into the back seat. Not being used to such a craft, we were all uneasy as we taxied down the runway, particularly since the door next to Bob would not stay shut. Our pilot told us not to worry, because up there, the air pressure would keep it closed. And behold, it did. It was thrilling to skim along just over the jungle canopy and watch the plane's shadow disperse livestock in the scattered *milpas*. At the grassy field near Palenque where the plane put down, an old derelict car was waiting to taxi us through a luxuriant tropical rain forest to the ruin.

Mexican archaeologists do not share the enthusiasm for life in the raw with some of their North American counterparts. The federal government, for whom most of them work, builds adequate housing facilities and hires a domestic staff before undertaking any excavations. Bob had made advance arrangements for us to use the unoccupied company house at Palenque. When I saw the enormous adobe stove that had to be fired with charcoal and knew that

I was supposed to be our kitchen help, I was glad that we had had the foresight to pack a primus burner and some army C-rations in our luggage. After such a gourmet lunch, the boys enjoyed romping in a lovely clear pool below the ruin called the Queen's Bath. Later in the moonlight, we strolled in total solitude through the clearing in front of the great pyramids that were topped with their massive sculptured temples. It was awe-inspiring, yet eerie. Not even the most calloused beings could have ignored the haunting probe of a thousand long-departed Mayan eyes peering through the blackened doorways.

The next morning, a Mexican family on holiday joined us for a descent to the famous tomb through the core of the largest pyramid. The caretaker started a motor, turned on a line of low-wattage lights that had been installed along the stairway, opened the metal grating over the stairwell, and departed. We moved noisily down the steep limestone steps that were very slippery from the excessive humidity of the damp air that had been trapped in the narrow shaft. As we were about halfway down, the lights flickered and then went off. We paused, waiting in vain for them to come back on, and then moved back up toward the entrance for fresh air. There were still no lights. The Mexicans shrugged and made their way out, but we did not. We had come too far and waited too long to give up so easily. Ever resourceful, Bob got out his Zippo pipe lighter. With its faint flame barely penetrating the gloom, we cautiously continued our descent. Each adult held onto a child to prevent him from slipping on the slimy rocks and crashing to the bottom. Much of the way, we slid downwards on our seats. It got blacker and blacker. I was reminded of Carlsbad Caverns, where the rangers turn off the lights momentarily to demonstrate the total darkness that occurs beneath the earth's surface.

From drawings in archaeological reports, Bob remembered that at the base of the stairs, there was an outer chamber off to the right. At one side of that, a doorway opened into the burial room itself. Gingerly probing in the very dim light with our hands and feet, we slowly moved into it. The priestly sarcophagus and its riches had long since been removed and transferred to the National Museum in Mexico City. The outer stone box, elaborately carved with Mayan glyphs, remained in place, nearly filling the tiny chamber. The air was hot, stale, and oppressive. Quite literally, it was deathly quiet. With a quick survey and a feeling that our mission had been accomplished, we were ready to make a hasty retreat.

Carved sarcophagus in tomb at base of the Temple of the Inscriptions
pyramid at Maya site of Palenque

Ascent was rapid as we thankfully moved toward the daylight at the entrance. Bob reached up to push open the metal grate. It was locked. We were
trapped inside the pyramid. Not realizing that he was dealing with foolish archaeologists, the caretaker had thought that everyone sensibly left when the
generator failed. We yelled and banged on the grating, hoping that he would
hear us and return with the key, but there was no response. I sat down on a
wet step, trying not to panic and trying not to look down into the black hole
from which we had just emerged. This predicament had to rank right up there
with the curse of the Pharaohs. After getting our second wind and becoming
thoroughly desperate, everyone yelled again and again, but our echoes were
swallowed up in the vastness of the setting. Then, just as we had almost given
up hope, a figure loomed darkly over us. It was an Indian who had been hired

to keep the jungle from engulfing the structures who finally heard our plaintive cries for help.

The return journey back to central Mexico began on schedule. The decrepit taxi and the plane with the broken door arrived as planned. Back at the empty Villahermosa airport, half an hour before the Aeronaves plane was due to arrive, I gave the boys their Dramamine pills. The agent on duty then announced that the connecting flight to Campeche would be two hours late. To kill time, we walked to a nearby park where two gigantic stone heads, excavated by our old friend, Matt Sterling, were on display. They were thought to be of Olmec origin and several thousand years old. The caretaker refused to open the gate, patiently explaining that it was Holy Thursday. We told him that we only wanted a quick look, that we promised not to take any pictures, and that we would leave quietly. He emphatically said no, that it was Holy Thursday. Defeated, we trudged back to the still empty airport. The boys were cross and hungry. Thankfully, they kicked some old fly-speckled newspapers off a bench and stretched out to sleep off the Dramamine. Though no explanations were offered, our plane was twelve hours late in arriving. When it finally did come, our flight to Mexico City was calm, but instead of relishing the experience, the boys slept all the way.

At Home in the Southwest

Mesa Verde, which is located in south-western Colorado, is one of the loveliest spots in the entire country. Its high tablelands that are torn asunder by deep, steep-sided canyons are carpeted in the summer with low evergreens through which many protected mule deer and wild turkeys meander. In the fall it is covered by a glorious blanket of gold and russet oak that thrive beneath an unblemished dome of blue, and there is always a gentle fresh breeze. Unobstructed vistas open up in a 360-degree panorama from the craggy, snow-creased San Juan and La Plata Mountains in the north to the flat desert sea shimmering across the southern horizon, above which the isolated spire of Shiprock seems to drift. Modern Southwest-erners are so commonly surrounded by such natural grandeur that they risk becoming insensitive to it, and perhaps that was the case with the ancient Indians as well.

It was to explore and add to the knowledge of prehistoric communities on the top of the Mesa Verde, as well as to clear the ruins so that they could then be made available to a steadily increasing throng of visitors, that Bob conducted a University of Colorado archaeology field school at the park for four summers from 1952 through 1956. Each year our family would meet the students, who usually numbered about twenty to twenty-five, at the Boulder campus and then convoy them through South Park, over Wolf Creek Pass, down to Durango, and on to Mesa Verde. The field school quarters consisted of a former school-house, whose one classroom served as a dining room and study hall, and an adjacent bunkhouse. There were electricity, hot water, refrigeration—near lux-ury for a field situation. Our family had two bedrooms and a bath in what was considered to be the teacher's apartment. My domain was a large, well-equipped kitchen because once again, I functioned as the camp's cook.

I also had another role, which is now as outdated as Victorian etiquette. Remember that there used to be college administrators known as Deans of Women who felt that chaperones were needed for mixed student bodies? There were, they did, and I was one. I served in these two unsalaried capacities both at Mesa Verde and also during the program's week-long tours that we regularly took through the other ruins and contemporary Pueblos in the northern Southwest. It took a great deal of planning and iron will on my part to travel all day, arrive at some chosen stopping place, set up camp and kitchen, and get a hot meal served before general mutiny had erupted. I was quickly cured of any unsuspected yearning I might ever have had to operate a restaurant.

The boys spent their days with the playmates they found among the Park Service families. They hiked, hung around the hitching rack for occasional free rides, visited the lodge soda fountain, explored, and enjoyed the games of childhood. Now and then they also went with the excavation crews to watch the tumble of fallen masonry walls being cleared and the trash mounds located to the south of every community being dissected for the discards of human activity, including burials. Not surprisingly, they were more fascinated by the stray rattlesnakes that had to be eliminated from the diggings. At night we observed Navajo teams going through a sterile reenactment of tribal dances for the benefit of park visitors. It was a week into our first season before I realized that an abrupt cliff fell off a few hundred yards from the schoolhouse. Nevertheless, I let the boys go on their way, hoping that they, like the Anasazi youngsters long before them, had enough common sense not to stray too close to the precipice.

Bob closed down his field school operations during the course of a large, long-term government excavation project on Wetherill Mesa, one of the arms of the plateau. He continued to be involved with Mesa Verde research as a member of a National Park Service advisory board. By this time, Frank and Gary were beginning to want their summers to be different. Some of their friends went to camp, but they wanted to experience the fun of staying at home to enjoy Little League baseball, swimming, biking, and other activities in which they had not yet been able to participate. I felt selfish in denying them these pleasures.

In 1965 Bob returned to set up the Mesa Verde Research Center, which he directed through 1970. During their high school years each of the boys put in a season as a digger—as their father told them, being paid to get in shape for football. Frank went on to work as a seasonal ranger and ultimately as the director of a program undertaken by the Ute Mountain Ute Indian tribe to stabilize the cliff ruins on their reservation, which adjoins Mesa Verde National Park. Meantime, I had taken a position at Boulder as a research librarian for the High Altitude Observatory and later for the National Center for Atmospheric Research.

In the old days we always used to laugh when Don Watson, the park's naturalist, told his stock joke at campfire talks, saying that if you wanted to see the best collection of Mesa Verde artifacts, you should just visit it the next time you were in Helsinki. Behind what might seemed to have been an odd comment were two facts. One was that until the Wetherill Mesa Project began, the park museum had to rely primarily on loans by private holders of artifacts that had been collected in surrounding finds because only a limited amount of modern field work had been done in the park itself. Secondly in the early 1890s, a young Swede named Gustaf Nordenskiold, assisted by the Wetherill brothers who are generally credited with making the cliff dwellings known, dug in a number of the sites; amassed a collection of various kinds of objects; and disregarding protests by the local citizens, sent the whole collection to Stockholm. Within two years Nordenskiold produced the first scientific account of the dwellings, including photographs of some of the ancestral Pueblo artifacts that had incongruously ended up in Europe. He died shortly thereafter, at which time his collection was purchased and given to the people of Finland.

In 1983 Bob and I finally followed Watson's advice. While on a tour of Scandinavia, we examined those well-traveled remains as part of the background research for a book dealing with Nordenskiold and with the journal he kept of his trip to the Far West, *Stones Speak and Waters Sing*. Apparently of no interest to the Finns, the Mesa Verde pots, baskets, and sandals had been immediately relegated into the same kind of obscurity that they had enjoyed before the ruins were discovered. For eighty years they were never taken out of museum storage and put on display. Subsequently, a few items were returned to Mesa Verde on temporary loan as part of an exhibit commemorating the centennial of Nordenskiold's explorations.

THE SERIOUS SIDE

During my summers at Mesa Verde, I made it a practice to spend several evenings a week working at tables piled with the pottery coming from the student digs, but most of my ceramic analysis was accomplished during the long winter days at the university. There a basement space located under the heating pipes and as gloomy as the catacombs was made available to me. I worked without financial compensation, merely trying to help my husband and also give myself a needed break from household chores and children's escapades.

The Mesa Verde pottery, which was my responsibility to classify, describe, and tabulate, comfortably conformed to taxonomic schemes already devised by others. I undertook this task by using the sight recognition methods I had been taught. As had been true with the Chaco pottery during my college experience, a remarkable conservatism on the part of the potters allowed the thousands of fragments made during some four centuries of continual potting to be sorted into half a dozen groupings. It was equally intriguing to note that although individual elements were shared by other contemporary Puebloan ancestors, the Mesa Verdeans slowly combined them in such a way as to produce a readily identifiable style. The sequence of Mesa Verde pottery with which I worked began with gray, smooth, banded, and corrugated cooking and storage jars and thin-walled service vessels coated with white engobe, over which was painted a rather standardized set of geometrics. These elements tended to be bolder and less varied than those of the previous eras, as though the potters had reached their stride after a long internship in the craft and were no longer interested in experimentation. Shapes were similarly limited, the most frequent of which being bowls of several sizes, pitchers, and ladles. All were useful in the low-level farming lifestyle of these people. As the culture moved to a climax, new form variations appeared. The most unique of these was a flat-bottomed mug with a single handle. One might assume that the Anasazi who lived north of the San Juan River in southwestern Colorado and southeastern Utah enjoyed some sort of beverage or liquid food that required such a vessel while those peoples dwelling to their south did not. For unknown reasons, the potters changed their methods from using a decorative pigment made from mineral oxides to a solution derived from the boiled extract of the Rocky Mountain beeweed. The effect was a lustrous black pattern that gleamed over a well-polished white slip. Balanced designs were densely massed, broad-lined, angular geometrical designs played off against some curvilinear elements. Flattened rims carried encircling round dots spaced around their circumferences. Rare and charmingly conceived painted or modeled animal figures, such as lizards, birds, or quadrupeds, enlivened the pottery in an appealing way.

Tree-ring dating was very successful in the Mesa Verde area. The dry environment preserved many wooden roof elements in the cliff houses, and datable charcoal was comparatively abundant in the old structures that were placed in the open. That, in turn, enabled scientists to formulate a sound chronology of the development and use of recovered pottery types throughout the ages. Ceramic classifications such as mine, taken together with the information accrued about architecture and other material advancements, therefore almost routinely allowed site after site to fit into a broadly sketched reconstruction of a civilization that slowly evolved at one place and then dissipated to regroup elsewhere.

REFERENCES

Lister, Robert H. and Florence C. Lister. *The Earl H. Morris Memorial Pottery Collection; An Example of Ten Centuries of Prehistoric Ceramic Art in the Four Corners Country of Southwestern United States.* University of Colorado Studies, Series in Anthropology, No. 16. Reprinted as *Anasazi Pottery.* Albuquerque: University of New Mexico Press, 1969, 1979.

Lister, Robert H., with a Chapter on Pottery by Florence C. Lister. *Contributions to Mesa Verde Archaeology: I. Site 499, Mesa Verde National Park, Colorado.* University of Colorado Studies, Series in Anthropology, No. 9. In *"Pottery"*, 47–62. Boulder: University of Colorado Press, 1964.

In the late 1950s most researchers believed that the northwestern border of Anasazi culture was the natural barrier of the mighty Colorado River. Limited reconnaissance explorations discovered a gradual abating of Mesa Verde–style remains as one moved west across southern Utah toward the river. A distinct, less advanced society occupied the opposite bank. In northern Arizona east of the Colorado, there was a localized variation of prehistoric Pueblo culture known as Kayenta. Up until now there had never been any definitive archaeological survey made on either the eastern or the western approaches to the river due to the extremely inhospitable geography of the river gorge itself and the wounds of exposed naked rock contracting away from it. Very likely the general territory would have remained as archaeological *terra incognita* had it not been for the construction of the Glen Canyon Dam and the great lake that would be impounded behind it. River waters were expected to back up some 185 miles from the dam site, reach depths of three hundred to four hundred feet in narrow stretches of the main canyon, and extend into numerous side tributaries that had eaten out their own sheer-walled declivities. In the modern era too much water would be a problem where formerly there had been too little, and the few Indian ruins that had been known since the late nineteenth-century John Wesley Powell explorations would be totally submerged. The University of Utah received Federal support to launch a comprehensive search-and-rescue program on both banks of the Colorado River north of its junction with the San Juan River, and the Museum of Northern Arizona undertook a comparable project on the eastern bank south of the San Juan. Salvage archaeology, which became the mainstay of Southwestern studies as energy-related activities brought a second opening of the West, was under way.

In 1957 Bob signed on as leader of the University of Utah survey team that was assigned to the western bank. Beginning at Wahweap, now a marina on Lake Powell, he and his workers commenced the long, arduous trek up the river and its side canyons toward Hite at the proposed lake head. Going by Jeep where feasible, by horse when motor transport was out of the question, and most often, by foot, they entered a territory that to a large extent was unknown except to a few uranium prospectors and river rats who had strewn vestiges of their dreams in out-of-the-way places.

The Glen Canyon world quickly overwhelmed Bob and his companions. It was violent in its contorted, weirdly weathered, and vividly colored strata, yet tranquil in the cool oases of seeping water, which were shadowed by high cliffs and encouraged clumps of trees to take root and maidenhair ferns and rock moss to cling to the sides of clear pools. In the summer it was torrid due to the relentless reflection off treeless walls of rock, but the men knew that it could also be frigid in winter, as the cliffs blocked out the sun. It was silent in the absence of human presence, yet alive with the sounds of nature. It was as removed from man's workaday world as any spot in America, and yet, despite this isolation, vapor trails from jets were constantly redesigning the sky overhead.

Possessing the physical stamina and keen powers of observation necessary for successful field archaeologists, the surveyors recorded campsites; places where hunters had paused to chip stone weapons; pictograph panels on stone facades; small granaries that had been used for storing wild seeds or the harvests from a patch of corn planted on river terraces; and here and there, a few two- or three-room houses tucked along the talus slopes that spilled down the heights. Although it was obvious that the river system had not been an unconquerable obstacle for the ancients, their utilization of the region on or near the waterways was limited and in many instances, probably seasonal. Nevertheless, with their simple lifestyles and ability to adapt, they had survived in a zone almost totally rejected by those who would follow them.

Archaeological interpretations are based upon the kind of deductive logic that is used in police detective work, but seldom do the two occupations interact. One deals with the present or recent past, the other with a time long before the reach of the statute of limitations. In Bob's first season on the Glen Canyon survey, however, he unexpectedly became involved both with the law and with a twenty-year-old mystery.

As his crew outfitted at the Mormon hamlet of Escalante, which was the departure point for treks to the Crossing of the Fathers, to Hole in the Rock, or to the rest of that portion of the Colorado River canyonlands, he was told repeatedly to be on the look-out in the areas where he was going for any evidence of a Los Angeles youth, Everett Ruess, who had vanished there in the late 1930s. Search parties had been mounted shortly after his disappearance. One of them had found the mules that Ruess had purchased from a local farmer, but no one saw a trace of the man or his property. Inevitably there were many theories about what had happened to this traveler whose existence had seemingly been erased from the human chronicles in the immensity of southeastern Utah. Perhaps he drowned while attempting to cross the roily river, as he had told a shopkeeper he intended to do in order to make his way down into the Navajo Reservation. Perhaps he fell from a cliff or was injured in some other accident that caused him to die alone in the wilderness. The most frequently expressed idea, conjured up in the suspicions of a tiny inbred village, was that the young man had happened upon a cattle rustling outfit that did him in. Local names were whispered as persons who likely knew more than they admitted.

To Bob, it was an interesting bit of local history, but one that he quickly forgot. That is, he forgot about it until one day a member of his party, who was working his way way down a canyon several miles from where the Ruess mules had been rounded up, spotted the word "Nemo" scratched on some rocks. Ruess had used the name of the Jules Verne character as a *nom de plume* on some of the sketches he had made during his wanderings. Shortly after this discovery, the surveyors paused for lunch in the coolness of an overhanging bluff. As they sat down in the shallow shelter, the gleam of a piece of metal protruding from beneath a boulder caught their sharp eyes. After dragging it loose, they discovered that it had been a smashed round canteen whose flannel covering had deteriorated. This was quite obviously a modern relic and just the sort of thing a desert traveler would have carried.

With the Ruess mystery now very much on their minds, the crew began turning over other rocks and poking about in the dirt and the talus. Slowly an assortment of other non-Indian items came to light. Most of them seemed to have been intentionally hidden. These included some hardened tubes of oil paint that an artist would have used, some scraps of cloth, a spoon, and a partially filled jar of Mentholatum with an Owl Drug Company of Los Angeles label. Spurred on by a feeling of being hot on the trail of an intriguing case, the surveyors were disappointed when they found no other clue about the owner of these stashed articles.

Back in Escalante, the finds were turned over to the County Sheriff. He promised to follow up on the matter and swore all of the concerned parties to secrecy until his investigations had been completed. A scenario of events was created that had Ruess being murdered as he camped in the explored alcove. His possessions had been crushed and concealed beneath the rock fall and his body thrown into the river several miles away. To confuse the searchers, the mules had been driven up and over into another canyon far removed from the crime scene.

Despite the secrecy pledge that Bob knew he and his associates had respected, he was besieged the very next day with comments from the locals about the finds. Some persons relayed to him that outlandish tales were being circulated about a cache of Ruess oil paintings having been recovered, miraculously unharmed by two decades of exposure to the elements. Others said that arrests were sure to follow, that so-and-so's cousin was doubtlessly implicated. Under the circumstances, Bob felt certain that such a long time had passed since the

Ruess disappearance that there would now be no interest in stirring up old troubles among kith and kin. Even though the routine of his immediate task had been broken by this uncommon excitement, he was relieved to move on to other, more ancient mysteries whose solutions would cause no pain.

Deciding to excavate an old village twenty miles northeast of Escalante as a field school activity, Bob returned there in the summers of 1958 and 1959. The boys and I accompanied him during the first season. The site was located in the fields of the farming community of Boulder, a cluster of houses and corrals in a verdant hanging valley, whose backdrop was a high evergreen mountain range and at whose feet lay an eroded mass of slick rock that had come sliding down in successive tiers toward the Colorado River. The area would never be flooded by Lake Powell, but Jesse D. Jennings, the archaeological project director, felt that clearing this largest regional site would yield information pertinent to an understanding of other contemporary remains.

During the duration of the school excavations, I again cooked for the group. This time, however, the kitchen was set up in a tent adjacent to the basement of an unfinished house that served as a workroom. The boys found entertainment among the children of the town, who introduced them to farm animals and machinery. Later in the summer, they and I retired to a shoddy motel in Escalante while Bob and the survey party resumed their taxing assignment. When fall arrived, we took our notes and artifacts to Salt Lake City, where we commenced with the laboratory analysis and report writing. I assumed the job of examining the ceramics from Bob's dig and ultimately, over a four-year period, all of the ceramics recovered by the entire Utah project. For the first time in my long involvement with pottery, I was finally on the payroll. Dr. Florence would have been proud. I, on the other hand, felt inadequate.

Many times during those early years, despite what I saw as my domestic obligations and privileges, I wished that I could finish my degree that had been interrupted by marriage and by the war, but I never seemed to have the time, the money, or the opportunity. No regional school then offered a doctorate in anthropology, and as the years passed, it seemed less and less important to my well-being. I therefore settled for auditing classes in anthropology, art history, and Spanish. That meant that the classes had to be at hours—usually during the late afternoons—when Bob's schedule allowed him to be home with the children. No latchkey kids here. I would rush home to put in several harried hours working in the kitchen or on other maternal chores and then collapse, wondering if it had all been worth it.

Finally being offered the chance of doing something professional in ceramics, I sought the help of Anna Shepard, our neighbor a block away to whom we had been introduced by Earl Morris. Like him, Anna lived and worked out of her Boulder home for the Carnegie Institution of Washington. Bob had previously arranged for Anna to teach several graduate seminars in ceramic analysis, a field in which she was considered to be the top specialist. These seminars were not successful, however, because Anna had little tolerance for those who did not share her broad background in the physical sciences of chemistry, mineralogy, and archaeology; and she seemed incapable or unwilling to come down to the students' level. After trying to absorb a plethora of facts and observations from her definitive book, *Ceramics for the Archaeologist,* I walked to her home for a series of training sessions with no small degree of trepidation.

The workroom to which she led me was a dingy cubicle off to one side of her living room that was cluttered with a jumble of sample boxes, equipment, notes, and publications. She pushed aside this overflow of ongoing research, and we went to work. Probably out of deference to my husband, Anna was patient, although doubtlessly sorely tried by my ignorance, and she slowly introduced me to the microscopic observations of the pottery substances and to the means of identifying them. This added a new dimension to my efforts, which had previously been limited to the considerations of surface physical characteristics and style—the generally accepted approach of most people then doing pottery studies. Now, however, I felt that I was getting into step with a new thrust forward in analytical ceramic research.

At the time of our contact with Anna, she was in her fifties. She was plain in appearance, colorless in personality, and ill at ease when out of her element. I attributed the latter to her years of caring for two ailing elderly parents and having little social life of her own. Her extreme shyness was apparent on a number of occasions when we tried to include her in affairs that we thought she would enjoy, for example, a gathering after a lecture by a visiting scholar. Invariably, she would phone at the last minute with some excuse for not coming. Following the death of her parents, she remained in the old family home that had gone many years without attention, both inside and out. I was convinced that she probably lived entirely on Campbell's soup, tuna salad, and scrambled eggs, spending all of her time concentrating on thin sections of pottery under her scope. Her work, which is still considered to be a landmark contribution, was her salvation, but all things considered, it seemed to me a high price to pay.

The other woman with whom I was associated during this period was Dee Ann Suhm (Story). She had finished her undergraduate training in Texas with Alex Krieger, the most eminent lithic specialist at that time, and her doctoral work at UCLA. We had met when she was hired to set up and direct the archaeological laboratory for the University of Utah's portion of the Glen Canyon project.

Typical of the times, Dee Ann came to work each day in high heels and dresses that she sometimes protected with a white lab coat. Efficient, knowledgeable, and comfortable in the traditional woman's role of bringing order to the masses of artifacts, photos, and notes pouring in from surveys and excavations, she nevertheless longed to participate in some of the field operations. In her heart, she really wanted to be a field researcher, but she also recognized the restrictions placed upon her gender's ability to do so. Jennings, the project director, was reluctant to authorize an active role for her in the field. He did not question Dee Ann's qualifications to direct such work, but he felt that the physical conditions of the Colorado River drainage were too difficult for females and that a lone woman in an otherwise all-male crew would be disruptive. This attitude should not be construed as hostility toward women in archaeology, but rather it came from a deep-seated respect for the fairer sex, which, whether acknowledged or not, put a damper on equal opportunity. As a special bonus, he eventually allowed Dee Ann to participate in several weeks of digging during the course of a multi-year endeavor.

After the Glen Canyon archaeological work ended, Dee Ann joined the faculty at the University of Texas at Austin. There she taught, ran the archaeological laboratory, and earned a highly deserved reputation for the annual field schools that she conducted in various parts of the state. As sexual distinctions in clothes and careers narrowed, however, she probably did so with fewer high heels and skirts.

THE SERIOUS SIDE

The Coombs Site, which was excavated by Bob, his students, and Dick Ambler; named for the property's owner and later made into Anasazi State Park, was a composite community of surface masonry and jacal structures and pithouses. In all, there were some fifty dwellings and about three dozen storage units. Surprisingly, the pottery, as well as the heterogeneous architecture and other features, indicated that it had basically been a colony of people who were allied with the Kayenta variation of ancestral Pueblo culture.

Using recovered pottery that had been dated in the Kayenta district, we postulated that the Coombs Site had been occupied from about A.D. 1075 to 1275. The colony had apparently finally been abandoned after a raging fire swept through the settlement. It was mind-boggling to contemplate the original feat of people getting their worldly goods, including fragile bulky pottery, over the rugged intervening terrain and across a treacherous river without the aid of draft animals, wheeled conveyances, or watercraft. It was yet another case of human backs and wills accomplishing wonders that were repeated continually throughout the span of the village's life.

Much of the Kayenta pottery was the usual Anasazi gray and black-on-white modes with certain regional characteristics. There was also a distinctive bright red style that often carried polychromatic decorations in red, orange, and black. Not unexpectedly, potters of the Coombs village, by virtue of being cut off from a customary source of supply, made imitations of these types. They clung to some techniques long after they had gone out of style among more centrally located Anasazi. Even though they lived in what must have been considered the Indian boondocks, the residents acquired some prehistoric earthenwares from as far away as Mesa Verde and Chaco Canyon, as well as from the Fremont pottery-producing Indians who lived nearby to their north.

Putting my Shepard tutoring to use, I observed that Kayenta potters preferred sand for gray and white wares, with the addition of crushed potsherds for reds. Mesa Verdeans generally used crushed rock for all of their varieties. Pottery from the sector known as the San Juan Triangle, lying east of the Colorado and north of the San Juan, substantiated the notion that the area had in fact been a Mesa Verde frontier. Some exchange with Kayenta potters was evident, although none could be ascertained with Fremont sources in eastern Utah.

The pottery of the three branches of the Colorado Plateau's prehistoric Pueblos that I was studying—Chaco, Mesa Verde, and Kayenta—had all come from interrelated, discretely defined cultural, temporal, and locational florescences. It had been made by the same hand-coiling methods, it bore a basically geometrical repertory composed of identical elements that had been inspired by the angular landscape around the artisans, it had been fired in the same ways, and it had ultimately served in many of the same functions. Other than some minor trade between the eastern Anasazi and the Mogollon to their south, some equally minor exchange between the northwesternmost Anasazi and the Fremont to their north. and a probable Mexican derivation a millennium earlier, there had been no intrusive interaction.

REFERENCES

Lister, Florence C. Pottery Analysis. In "The Glen Canyon Archaeological Survey" by Don D. Fowler. *Anthropological Papers of the University of Utah,* No. 39, 22–25, 1959.

———. Pottery. In "The Coombs Site" by Robert H. Lister. *Anthropological Papers of the University of Utah,* No. 41, Pt. I, 66–90, 1959b.

———. Pottery. In "The Coombs Site" by Robert H. Lister. *Anthropological Papers of the University of Utah,* No. 41, Pt. II, 182–238, 1960.

———. Pottery. In "The Coombs Site" by Robert H. Lister. *Anthropological Papers of the University of Utah,* No. 41, Pt. III, 32–90, 1961.

———. "Kaiparowits Plateau and Glen Canyon Prehistory: An Interpretation based on Ceramics." *Anthropological Papers of the University of Utah,* No. 71, 91 pp., 1964.

Off to Africa

To students of ancient history, readers of the Bible, or viewers of Hollywood epics, the mere mention of the Nile evokes visions of exotic pageants of former life that, with all their lushness and innate mysticism, seem far removed from this time and place. Certainly Southwestern archaeologists never contemplated any connection of their work with that branch of science known as Egyptology. In that sphere many aspects of an advanced human civilization that had been developed by thousands emerged, while a handful of transients moving through the Southwest were still concerned with day-to-day survival using their wooden atlatls.

Another dam-building project, however, propelled several teams from Colorado and Texas deep into what was both a historical record that extended back in time some five thousand years and also a prehistory reaching into the nether regions beyond those many millennia, perhaps even to the emergence of genetically modern man. This was the Aswan High Dam that was being erected in the early 1960s over an older lower dam at the First Cataract. It would impound waters from the mighty Nile southward through a desolate area known as Nubia to as far as the Second Cataract in the Republic of the Sudan.

Unlike the generally unoccupied locale of the Glen Canyon Dam, the thin strip of arable Nubian land beside the Nile had been continuously used by humans for eons. Now, however, scores of residents were to be evacuated along what was to be the flood level of the anticipated Lake Nasser, and their towns would slowly be relinquished to a watery grave. In addition, another fifty major known antiquities, such as Philae, which was located on an island already seasonally inundated, and the two temples of Abu Simbel farther upriver would also be sacrificed or moved from their original settings in the name of progress. Nubia, to the south of Upper Egypt proper, had been a source of resources and manpower throughout the history of dynastic Egypt, particularly after the Middle Kingdom established its capital at Thebes. Because there was little or no archaeological knowledge of perhaps thousands of smaller sites along the lifeline of the river, the governments of Egypt and the Sudan, aided by the U.S. and other countries, sent an appeal around the world for scientific help and salvage. "Save the Monuments of Nubia" became a veritable battle cry! Antiquities that had in some cases lain undisturbed for thousands of years needed to be summarily explored.

The archaeologists at the University of Colorado were among those chosen from a dozen institutions to represent their responding countries. In 1962 they received a concession from the Sudanese authorities to explore any encountered remains that lay within a prescribed square mile on the western bank of the Nile opposite the northern Sudanese regional commercial center of Wadi Halfa. Within this sector, there were several modern settlements located along a narrow stretch of loam beside the river, which were destined to become vacated, and also some known remnants of older cultures under drifted sand nearby. No one knew for certain what they might find in the unexplored, terraced, rocky expanses extending off to the western horizon. Although none of the Colorado scientists were expert in dealing with the large constructions, hieroglyphics, statuary, or material culture of the ancient Egyptians, they reasoned that their Southwestern experience in excavating the small mud brick village clusters left by simple farmers who were trying to cope with an arid environment would be applicable.

Bob assumed the administrative directorship of the Colorado effort during its second season of 1963–1964. I took on the task of analyzing the ceramics from the first two periods of excavation. These focused upon the sedentary occupations when pottery-making and earthenware utilization had been important cultural adjuncts. Before making any firm commitments, however, as always we had a family council. We had to be certain that the boys understood what their sacrifices and benefits would be, since we felt that they were old and responsible enough at ages fifteen and twelve to have a say about their lives. If they rejected the project, so would we. They would have to miss a whole year of school. That would put them out-of-step with the friends with whom they had begun first grade, but by going on this trip, they would be rewarded with the matchless educational experience of a year's travel around the world. To our relief, we found that we had sufficiently brainwashed them over the years so that they eagerly agreed to join the expedition.

In August 1963, we set sail from New York on the German liner, the *Bremen*. Bob could scarcely forget that the one previous time he had gone to Europe by ship was to fight those very Germans. This time, however, the enemy was seasickness, as rough seas, which were announcing the approach of the hurricane season, quickly demonstrated to us that the ship's stabilizers were not the solution to all of our problems. Gratefully, we made a landfall seven days later off of Southampton and began a two-month tour of Europe and its many landmarks, ruins, inns, museums, and sidewalk cafes.

Both of the boys were also eager to take it all in. Lest this sound like complete gaiety and light, however, let me say that any prolonged travel by parents together with their offspring places severe strains on familial relationships, especially at times when hunger or fatigue take over. Nevertheless, I can proudly proclaim that an uprooted year that was begun afloat on the *Bremen* bound us together in our small travel victories and defeats and created among us an exceptionally close family bond that has endured into the boys' maturity.

Headed for a rendezvous with our party in Cairo, which, when all assembled, numbered twenty-eight men and women and a few children, we arrived from Greece one evening in late October. As we took the limousine ride from the airport to our hotel, we soon realized that we had entered into a world that was at least superficially very different from our own. Noisy swarms of men and boys, many wearing the traditional ticking-striped *jellaba* robes and loose turbans that seemed about to unwind, elbowed their way along the streets or sat at sidewalk tables smoking water pipes or drinking hot tea from murky glasses. Horse-drawn carts competed with large American automobiles for space on the streets, each contributing its own kind of pollution. Here and there, soldiers armed with machine guns stood aloof from the crowds.

The few days we had set aside for sightseeing and for familiarizing ourselves with the local scene sped by, as we rushed from museum to pyramids and from bazaars to mosques. This is not the recommended way to visit monuments of great importance. One should first have background information, then a proper frame of mind, and finally, sufficient time and solitude to put the data and impressions in order. Regrettably, the rapid transit of modern travel does not allow for leisurely absorption. Under these circumstances, our reactions were those of wonder at the skill and imagination of ancient crafts-men, disappointment over the relatively small dimensions of the Sphinx, amazement at the volume of the man-made piles to honor a single individual, and interest in the potters at work in Fustat who were pulling vessels out of inert clay with deceptive casualness. Also we experienced a profound cultural shock, since we were not yet and never would become accustomed to the clamor, the filth, or the aggressive push-and-shove and give-me mentality that surrounded us.

Two days before we were to head south, Bob received word that there were problems concerning our field equipment at the Egyptian customs office. Sealed barrels and boxes of gear had been shipped in bond from Piraeus, Greece, with the understanding that they would be dispatched directly through Egypt to the Sudan without having to be inspected. Now apparently, that was not to be the case. The first clue indicating that there might be trouble ahead came when the guards at the custom office refused to allow Bob entrance so that he could determine the nature of the difficulty. It was obvious that they were eye-ing the pleasure of a pay-off from Bob so that he could get into a building to which he had formally been summoned. That not being forthcoming, they sullenly allowed him entrance after considerable haggling.

Then it was a sojourn from official to official, with long, pointless waits in-between, and each person avowing that he was only trying to help while si-multaneously throwing up one administrative roadblock after another. Either the papers were incomplete or incorrect, or there was no precedent, or per-haps a few changes or official seals could be added for a small fee. Take them here, take them there, get another signature, have another conference. Ulti-mately, Bob was convinced that this was a grand game of attrition of the spirit aimed at wearing him down to such a point of desperation that he would pay bribes, the accepted enrichment known as *baksheesh,* in order to get the gov-ernment officers to perform the jobs for which they presumably had been hired. Little did these Egyptians realize they had finally come up against one stub-born American who would outwit them! Not to be outdone, however, the Egyptians flatly announced during the late afternoon of the first day that all of the University of Colorado packages would have to be opened for inspection.

In the customs warehouse, a throng of presumed but non-uniformed helpers began to remove the strapping and pry open our barrels. Eager hands reached into everything and arbitrarily yanked articles out of the securing packing. The possibilities for damage and theft were enormous. Losing control of the situation, Bob was distraught. Nor did he feel at all comforted by the presence of an unfriendly man carrying an inventory list who stood to one side demanding an explanation for each item, apparently to determine that we were not smugglers or some other types of subversives. Bob recalled later that he had described an unfamiliar object as a "scientific instrument," which seemed to satisfy the inspector. Later he learned that it was a pipe tobacco reamer one of the students had pushed into the side of a box. Just when our equipment was in complete disarray, it was suddenly closing time. The barrels stood open and supplies were exposed or lying all over the floor. Ignoring Bob's protests, the officials decreed that everything had to be left as it was. Bob was sure that by the next morning our expedition would be stripped, but, fortunately, he was wrong.

Apparently having given up hope of any under-the-counter payment and wishing to expedite matters, the chief customs official released our goods with an imperious wave of the hand at the end of the second day. He told Bob that his men would oversee the shipment's removal to the railroad station in time for our departure that evening. By then, however, Bob would have none of it. He went out into the street in front of the customs house, commandeered a two-wheeled, horse-drawn cart, and with the help of several idle hangers-on, personally loaded our paraphernalia. All the while, he was simultaneously having to beat off other would-be assistants who had shoved in around him with their hands held out for money. Ignoring their screaming invectives and with Frank walking closely behind him, Bob escorted the cart of expedition gear by foot to the station through the congested streets of Cairo, passing along the way the towering statue of Ramses II, which was then being raised in an intersection parkway. Having done all he could just to reach the station, he then had to depend upon the baggage handlers to get the gear aboard the train. The nagging question was, would they?

We awoke the next morning to find that the train was chugging up the Nile

Valley, at that season flooded as far as the eye could see with the river's annual offering of enriching soils. By noon we had reached Luxor, or ancient Thebes. During the late afternoon, we were overwhelmed by the great verticality and volume of the pylons, columns, courtyards, and temples of Karnak. We then hired a *felucca* to sail us across the muddy, fast-flowing river. On the western bank, we hailed an antique, sputtering car that served as a taxi to take us farther west into the barren desert hills to the impressive palace of Queen Hatshepsut (1515–1484 B.C.) and to the famous but bleak *rincón* known as the Valley of the Kings. Over the course of a century of exploration, the tombs of the boy Pharaoh Tutankhamen and other nobility had been discovered there, plunged deep into the heart of several ridges to receive their royal offerings and then concealed with rock slides so that their treasures could not be stolen. In the early 1960s, the valley was still free of the depressing tangle of tourist concessions and the persistent strident salesmen hawking fake scarabs and statuettes that would later be prevalent there. We were alone except for a dozing, ragged caretaker, whose nap had been interrupted by our taxi driver. This guardian of the ages angled a large mirror at the entrance to King Tut's tomb for our benefit, so that the sun's reflected rays lighted up the sloping shaft down to the burial chamber. It had long since been emptied of its fabulous loot and, we hoped, cleansed of its alleged curse. This time, Bob's trusty Zippo lighter was not needed.

Returning to the train, we proceeded southward to Aswan. There we clawed our way onto an overcrowded local bus that was headed for the dock above the dam construction site, where the Nile steamer that was to take us the rest of the way to Wadi Halfa had been moored. One cultural trait that the British unfortunately failed to instill in their former colonies is that of the queue. Instead, any activity that in England would require lining up in an orderly single file is replaced in these countries by mayhem at its worst. We found Egypt to be no exception. All steamer passengers—including those who were ticketed with so-called first class accommodations as well as those who had no advance reservations, who expected to sleep outside on the lower deck, and who were carrying what seemed to be a large part of their worldly goods—were funneled through the same narrow entrance gate. It was survival of the fittest. We were assaulted, nearly maimed, pushed, and trampled upon just to board a crudely furnished, ultra-Spartan, double-decker river craft. Once on board, we dumped our suitcases into a hot stateroom that had two bunks and had recently been sprayed with Flit. Then we moved outside to the open stern deck to watch the suffering of others who were trying to accomplish this same feat. Feeling totally relieved at seeing our fought-over field equipment arrive, we drank our first partially chilled Camel beer. In more discriminating times, such a potent would have seemed almost unpalatable, but at that moment, it was a delight which Bob remembered with pleasure for the next twenty years.

As we sat sipping this nectar, we had our first glimpses of the kinds of people among whom we were to live for the next six months. The dark-skinned Nubian women, whom we had previously not seen, were fascinating to observe wearing their gauzy black outer garments, vividly colored dresses, and plastic Taiwanese thongs, and sporting brightly painted nails and facial tattoos. Perhaps even more than the men, they mirrored the centuries of Caucasoid and Negroid racial blending that had occurred along the Nile corridor from central Africa to the Mediterranean. One thing was certain. They did not live up to our preconceptions that they were docile, browbeaten, furtive females in fear of their lives from overpowering males. These ladies, as well as those we would later meet in Wadi Halfa, were shrill, extroverted, and openly curious. One got the impression that they were the masters of their homes, as indeed they had to be, since economic conditions forced their husbands to spend months of exiled servitude in Egypt.

The trip by steamer took a day-and-a-half and two nights traveling south from Aswan. The routine of activities on our deck was quiet and geared to mealtimes. Below, where the natives crowded in between bundles of cargo, it seemed to be much livelier, with instantaneous singing or drum-beating to break the monotony. As we slowly moved against the current, tiny sprinklings of cube-like houses stacked along rocky escarpments were barely visible against the sere, pale background that shimmered under a pitiless sun. Ragtag, barefoot boys stood in their tracks waving at the passing ship, as they had done twice a week all their lives. Here and there, a small apron of alluvium supported a few trees and patches of vegetables that were watered by an ageless balance-beam water lift, or *shaduf,* and tilled by wooden plows drawn by mixed teams of camels and oxen. Out beyond these oases lay unbroken seas of tan sand creeping unceasingly in duned waves toward any obstruction. In contrast to our American deserts, there was almost no vegetation or sign of living

Western landscape with natural pyramidal forms and a line of thin vegetation by the banks of the Nile south of the Aswan Dam prior to inundation by Lake Nasser

things. At several isolated villages, the ship pulled alongside the river banks while goods and mail were unloaded. These brief stays provided welcome breaks in the dreary daily cycle for folks who were about as far out on the fringe of the modern world as one could get.

On the second day just before reaching the border between Egypt and the Sudan, we floated right up to the beach in front of the four colossal statues of seated gods that were guarding the portal to the main monument of Abu Simbel. This was a hypostyle, hieroglyphic-covered temple, which had been thrust back some 180 feet into the living rock of a vertical cliff face on the Nile's western bank in ca. 1200 B.C. When it first gained the public's attention during the early 1800s, its entrance had been nearly hidden by great drifts of sand. The colored works of art inside the temple, however, had been exceptionally well-preserved. The vision behind such a construction, erected with enormous expenditure of time and labor to honor Ramses II and his pantheon of deities, stretches the imagination.

Even more intriguing was its purposeful location, which had been oriented in such a way, that for one fleeting moment twice a year, the rays of the rising sun shot like an arrow to the inner recesses of the rear chamber and fell as a

*Nile steamer floats up to the two facades of the Egyptian temple of Abu Simbel
prior to their elevation to the cliff top above the Nile River*

blessing upon the face of a waiting statue. Otherwise, the darkness and enormity of the hall served to instill a sense of somber reflection in all observers. Before the dam caused the waters of Lake Nasser to rise, Abu Simbel experienced a modern miracle equaling that of its creation, when it was removed in blocks to be repositioned at the crest of the cliff. It was shorn of its protective natural shell, but still faced the dawn.

That afternoon, as we continued on to the south, we witnessed one of the many glorious garnet-red sunsets that colored the western sky and would close many of our days ahead. Then up from the east came a round, white moon whose bright light washed over the elevations of hills and dunes while leaving their folds in deep shadow. The sharp contrast between the silvered watery highway of the great river and the solitary denuded desert on either side somehow symbolized the fabled mystery of the East. The boys remembered that back home it was Halloween, quite often a cold and blustery holiday with only make-believe spirits gadding about.

Wadi Halfa was an old town that had developed upon a narrow ribbon of

Downtown Wadi Halfa, northern Sudan, now under water

arable land on the eastern bank of the Nile. Situated at the northern entrance
to the 100-mile-long granitic impediment that formed the Second Cataract, it
was then and always had been a focal point for the occasional river traffic coming south from Egypt. We later observed that the railroad, which extended
south from Wadi Halfa to Khartoum, was being used to move the displaced
reluctant Nubian residents under a camel-mounted military guard. There was
no passable highway more than a few miles to the north and south. Several
dozen blocks of small businesses formed a *souk,* which was intertwined with
streets covered ankle-deep in sand. Many nondescript homes built flush on
the streets opened up around interior courtyards that were cluttered with the
accumulated debris of life. There were two mosques with loudspeakers over
which the recorded *muezzin*'s call to the faithful blared five times daily beginning at four in the morning. A neglected cemetery, with rocks and earthen pots
strewn over the graves and scrawny goats browsing through piles of trash, was
located nearby. On the southern edge of town was a hotel that catered to the
handful of adventuresome travelers who quickly passed through. No vegetation of any kind away from the river provided shade or softened the harshness.

*Wadi Halfa cemetery with pottery vessels, once containing food offerings,
before rough gravestones*

Out beyond town lay a small airport, which received mail twice a week and
which was embellished with a preposterous sign that read "Keep Off the Sand,"
as if one more footprint would have made any difference to such a doomed
speck on the map.

Although racial interbreeding between Africa's whites and blacks was generally very apparent, the populace of Wadi Halfa was basically Semitic. The
residents were predominately Muslim; however, there were also a few Coptic
Christians. Most Wadi Halfans were small tradesmen, craftsmen, government
workers, or seasonal domestics who worked in neighboring Egypt. Arabic was
the common language, but a broken English was spoken or understood by
many. We found the adults to be friendly and deserving of their reputation for
honesty. It was their children who were troublesome. Thanks to the corrupt-
ing influence of travelers, most had learned the two English phrases, "What is
your name?" and "Give me money." A lack of response to either—which for
the next six months greeted us the moment we emerged from our houses—
brought on a shower of rocks.

The Colorado party found rustic quarters in three houses, two of which were staffed by ancient male servants. In his youth our cook had served as a cook for the British armies in India and East Africa. Our other servant, a withered, sour-faced old fellow who waited tables and did some minimal cleaning, was proud to have served Churchill and Roosevelt at their wartime meeting in Casablanca. Bob soon became "Commander" to them both, and I became "Commander Lady."

Private rooms were put to use as sleeping quarters, and the open, roofed connecting spaces became dining and study rooms. Our kitchen was a separate cubicle at the rear of a small enclosed courtyard that allowed access to a side street. In the yard huge earthenware jars were placed on a stand to cool drinking water, and a sink and a tap had been installed for domestic use. A privy stood off to one side, and a shower stall had been placed on the other. There was electricity, and propane gas was used for cooking. Our refuse was collected by a honey-bucket system that invariably arrived on our block during the dinner hour. Our beds were wooden frames that had been laced with ropes.

The old saying about armies marching on their stomachs could just as easily apply to field parties. Food tends to become terribly important when there is little else to do for recreation. In the northern Sudan we were at a great disadvantage in this regard, since Wadi Halfa's nearly total isolation from supply sources, added to its limited local resources, made for extremely curtailed diets. Not only was there no pork allowed because of religious prohibitions, but there were also no beef or dairy products on the market either. No alcoholic beverages were available other than Greek ouzo and a local date brandy, both of which were definitely acquired tastes.

In addition to these natural shortages, the dwindling stocks in the small local stores had also not been replenished due to the prevailing atmosphere of the approaching evacuation. Somehow, however, we managed to survive on a meager diet consisting of a type of course, gritty bread that was often infested with weevils, which we tried to hide under coatings of mixed fruit jam or marmalade, goat meat, camel tongue, canned tuna, eggs, a few greens, eggplant, peanut soup, Nescafé or tea, and on special occasions, a heavy date pudding. It was an unenlivened cuisine guaranteed to assure that most of our table conversation dealt with the rich foods that we so longingly remembered. The consensus was that it was best not to visit the local open-air food market, the water works, or for that matter, even our own kitchen, since the sanitary conditions at these places were far from ideal and caused us unending intestinal problems. When a dispensary clerk at the socialized medical facilities handed me a full quart jar of diarrheal pills, I knew we were in for a very long winter.

It was just a matter of time until our party took on the appearance of a masquerade. Pith helmets, bush jackets, and desert boots sprouted up on all sides, as we enjoyed play-acting the roles of English movie-style archaeologists. Several were bold enough to appear at dinner in *jellabas,* but the jeers of their colleagues soon caused them to relegate those garments back to their footlockers. That was before we saw the French scientist, however, who cut a dashing and conspicuous swath wearing the baggy black bloomers and red cummerbund of an Algerian Tuareg, a costume no doubt inspired by a French Foreign Legion film.

The principal task of the University of Colorado project was to sample a complex of structures that had been erected on a low sandy bench above a narrow strip of fertile land at the river's edge, based on historical accounts believed to have been dated from the fifth through the tenth centuries. The site was surrounded by the mud houses of the modern community of Gezira Dabarosa. All that remained of the original town were the foundations and stubs of the adobe and stone walls of a small chapel and more than one hundred living rooms arranged in a maze-like compound. After its abandonment, the entire site had been covered with a thick dune of sand.

Back in Colorado it had sounded like a simple matter for us to go and excavate such a primitive agricultural community. Once on site, however, it was immediately obvious to us that adaptations for the unique local circumstances would have to be made. First, the shifting composition of the fill made it impossible to maintain clear stratigraphic controls, and it also caused the wheelbarrows, which were standard equipment on Southwestern digs, to mire down during the earth-moving process. Secondly, there was the matter of the available labor pool needed to clear the site under the direction of our staff. Because of the manpower needed by the many other international expeditions that were located in the vicinity of Wadi Halfa, the Sudanese authorities were forced to import hundreds of men from Khartoum. The antiquities office established a uniform pay scale for the workers and also created inflexible, high ratios of native field directors—who traditionally came from the Egyptian town of Kuft—to the number of workmen. All of these men lived in rude communal

*Kufti overseer of University of Colorado excavations of eighth-century village
on west bank of Nile opposite Wadi Halfa. Modern occupation in background*

camps that had been set up on the desert near the excavation sites on which
they worked. If we had been in the Southwest using Indian or other laborers,
our job could have been handled by several dozen men. In the Sudan, on the
other hand, it was impossible to get along with less than several hundred workers because of the relatively small amount of work that was accomplished by
any one person.

We therefore had to draw our work force from the two major and bitterly
opposing blocks of Sudanese society. One segment was composed of the blue-
black, pencil-thin Nilotic Negroes, who came from the southernmost part of
the country and who had been converted to Christianity by Catholic missionaries during the last century. The other group was that of the Semitic Muslims,
who dominated central and northern Sudan. The result of this unfortunate
mixture that had been forced upon us was an underground racial and religious
tension, which was kept at a near boiling point by the derogatory songs that
the men sang about each other as they worked and by the frequent scuffles
that daily threatened to erupt into full-scale riots. It was admirable inspiration

on the part of some of our students to step in and teach the men the football fighting songs of their two main alma maters, the Universities of Colorado and Michigan. The workers entered into the spirit of the songs, shouting out words they did not understand and at the same time, unknowingly adopting a faster tempo of work. "Glory, Glory Colorado" and "Champions of the West" translated into an uneasy peace and a greater productivity.

Another adjustment that our crew had to make was dictated by native habits. Shovels were tools that were unfamiliar to the laborers, and their usage required a set of manual movements that were difficult for them to master. Therefore, under the direction of the Kufties, who for several generations had specialized in clearing the Egyptian monuments, the typical excavation technique had become one of scraping sand forward into small baskets by using a broad, short-handled hoe. Larger objects fell free, but smaller ones were ignored. Then the baskets were carried on the shoulders of a procession that plodded continuously from dig to dump in the Pharaonic tradition of building pyramids.

Seeing sherds and who-knew-what-else being discarded with abandon in this haphazard removal process, our archaeologists, who were accustomed to scrupulously saving all artifacts no matter how small, became very distressed over the fact that this procedure was also customary for the native professionals in this particular field as well as for the helpers whom they groomed. Perhaps their unselective methods had resulted from having to work with the enormous quantities of cultural evidence that had been deposited here for many millennia, but we were determined not to be similarly seduced into such a careless handling of the archaeological record. One result of our more meticulous excavation procedures was that, where formerly only complete vessels had been considered, I made the first (and probably the last) tabulated sherd count for any site ever excavated in Lower Nubia.

At the outset, I had intended to cross the Nile each day with the student crew on an old U.S. Navy landing craft that our government had given the Sudan to use as a ferry, so that I could work on the pottery in the shade of a *ramada* that had been thrown up at the site. This proved to be impractical, however, due to the limited supply of available washing water, the annoying clouds of flies, and the intense glare off the surrounding sand that made close work very difficult. It therefore became necessary for the students to load themselves down each day with the accumulated plastic bags of sherds and bring them back to our house. Nancy Buckles, the wife of one of our graduate students, and I set up work tables in our backyard, and Gary became our sherd washer.

Frank was given the job of working as helper for the expedition's surveyor, Jerry Goebels. That was fine with Frank, since Jerry had been a first-string quarterback at the University of Michigan. The two of them took off each morning with the rest of the crew and walked over more of the Colorado concession—which started at the river bank and extended to the empty land stretching off to the west—than any of the rest of us.

Teams of students within our group concentrated on different cultural problems. One of the teams sought evidence of Paleolithic remains *in situ*. On the eastern side of the river, the surfaces of the uppermost terraces that had survived the preliminary channeling of the ancient Nile—now some three hundred feet above the present water level—were strewn with a fantastic assortment of heavy stone hand axes left by Old Stone Age hunters who had wandered through this area, then under savannah conditions, in search of resident game animals. There were no such deposits on the western bank, but diligent efforts did produce tables full of small Upper Paleolithic and Mesolithic stone points and chips that had been left by a much later population. These were analyzed and later reported upon by Henry Irwin, who had just completed a study of the Paleolithic period in southern France, and by Joe Ben Wheat, a Colorado associate.

Four other students worked on problems concerning human physical evolution or adaptation. They successfully found the graves of older Nile valley dwellers that were located almost under the front doors of the present houses. Their work inevitably drew a daily audience of children. We had feared that exhuming the burials might lead to protests from the nearby residents, but they were strangely unconcerned. The team studied the recovered remains, searching for information about racial admixtures, dentition, various endemic osteological illnesses, and other maladies.

Originally we had thought that the climatic aridity would help to retain skin tissue, nails, and hair on otherwise desiccated bodies. To the great disappointment of the physical anthropologists, however, their digging showed that, although they were seemingly dry, the sites were far too exposed for this kind of delicate preservation. Fortunately, burial materials that had been retrieved by other archaeological groups who were currently not interested in these matters were turned over to our group, helping them to fill out the record. At one time when our Volkswagen van brought thirty withered, twisted corpses that had been donated by the Scandinavian expedition back to our compound, we considered sending off a tongue-in-cheek advertisement to the company about the vehicle's roomy interior (Holds Up to Thirty Adults!) for some sort of nebulous compensation. A medium-rare steak, smothered in braised mushrooms and accompanied by a full-bodied red wine, would have been acceptable.

We had been in Wadi Halfa for three weeks when the assassination of President John F. Kennedy stunned the world. Garbled word of this tragedy reached us third-hand through servants who worked at the Southern Methodist University expedition house and had heard the report on the BBC morning news. Like those of our countrymen in the United States, our reactions went from disbelief, to dismay, to anger, and finally, to sorrow. These feelings were probably all intensified by our distance from home and by our inability to get immediate reliable information. We fruitlessly huddled around the one available shortwave radio, hoping to tune into the Voice of America broadcasts. Instinctively, we longed to be back home in the same way families do who are drawn together by an abrupt misfortune.

While our feelings about the horrible events were predictable, those of the Sudanese around us were surprising. Mohammed and Hassan, our uneducated domestic help, unhesitatingly blamed the Egyptians. Such a seemingly illogical conclusion can be attributed to a deep-seated Nubian resentment, the result of their years of being forced into an inferior economic and social status by their aggressive Egyptian neighbors. It was a psychological reflex reaction of the Nubians to regard the Egyptians as responsible for everything evil in the world.

The profound respect our young president had commanded abroad, however, even among these humble peasants whom one might have expected knew nothing of the larger world beyond their enclave on the Nile, was demonstrated repeatedly over the next few weeks. The servants asked us to have a cable of sympathy sent on their behalf to Mrs. Kennedy, for which they were willing to pay from their paltry weekly salaries. Such a message was dispatched in their names at the expedition's expense, and a reply was duly received several months later. Mrs. Kennedy had played an active role in the "Save the Monuments of Nubia" campaign, and the Nubians had not forgotten her. Sudanese officials, with whom we had dealings, and private citizens in the *souk* stopped us to express their regrets, as if we had personally known our leader. Their obvious sadness at our national trauma was a heart-warming prop that helped us get on with our jobs.

For the next four months the multi-faceted research being carried out by us and by other international groups continued to hold our interest. French and English groups were clearing the huge fortifications that had been erected at the Second Cataract during the Middle Kingdom dynasties several thousand years before Christ. These installations had been designed to protect the lengthy trade routes from central Africa, over which such luxuries as gold, alabaster, slaves, ostrich eggs, and leopard skins were transported to the opulent royal courts of Upper Egypt. Spaniards were searching for signs of an earlier cultural evolution that had perhaps extended back to Neolithic beginnings. Polish workers were removing larger-than-life polychrome murals from church walls. Some of our fellow Americans were digging in sixth-century towns. At the other end of the local cultural continuum, others were trying to ascertain the extent and the kind of a more nomadic Paleolithic utilization of the region.

Less academic diversions were few, once the novelty of the setting had eroded. There were some drum-beating and chanting ceremonies among the native female populations, which some members of our group felt bold enough to attend. There was an occasional soccer game, where barefoot players on a hard dirt surface skitted about like desert gazelles. Uncomfortable camel rides took us into the hills, reminescent of scenes from the movie, *Lawrence of Arabia.* We christened one beast "Old Faithful" because he periodically exploded into teeth-baring, strangling noises. Our many photographic excursions consumed dozens of rolls of film, and we had enough opportunity to read and reread the library of paperbacks that had accumulated as discards from the company baggage. Generally, however, we had to admit that our days of rest—Fridays, in keeping with Muslim practice—passed slowly.

Gary's plans for entertaining himself while contributing to the over-all project never quite jelled. Before we left Colorado, the university museum preparator had shown him how to preserve faunal specimens, hoping that he would obtain a sample study collection. With this purpose in mind, Gary built himself a cramped workroom at our quarters in Wadi Halfa, using the large, sturdy cardboard shipping boxes that had contained some of our expedition supplies. Because we had no permit to bring firearms into the country, Gary had ac-

Friday camel ride diversion into the rocky terraces east of Wadi Halfa in background

quired a wrist rocket. This was a modified slingshot that provided greater thrust. He faithfully practiced with this weapon, but never quite mastered it. That was immaterial, however, because there was a great dearth of wild animal life in this region due to the absence of natural foods and perhaps also due to centuries of human predators. Gary's catch was primarily limited to a few lizards, some of which he snared himself and some of which he enterprisingly bought from little boys who lived nearby. Then one day as we walked through the cemetery en route to photograph a creaking water wheel at the river's edge, he spotted a cinnamon-and-black bird sitting on the wall. It was a hoopoe, native to North Africa but unknown in the New World. Gary took aim with his wrist rocket, flung his stone, and the bird fell dead to the ground. At first stunned and then almost sick that he had hit a target, he nevertheless picked up his trophy and took it back to his laboratory, where he spent the next several days stuffing and preparing it as he had been instructed. Gary's hoopoe still likely resides in the University of Colorado museum.

Another potential addition to his collection was a viper that Bill Buckles suspected lived under a huge boulder at the site he was testing. This species of deadly snake was especially dangerous because it buried its body underneath

the sand and could not be seen before being stepped upon. Bill and Gary decided to try and outsmart this snake. They labored many evenings preparing a
trap, which they devised from a five-gallon petrol can. To their disgust, however, the viper never got the hang of it. Eventually they had to pursue him
more directly with a shovel and a jar of formaldehyde.

After the several clusters of modern dwellings on the western bank had
been evacuated and their owners had been removed to the steppes east of Khartoum, a group of us decided to make an inspection tour of the deserted
houses. We soon learned that going into buildings that had been homes for
several generations until just a few weeks ago was very different than poking
through a long-deserted archaeological site or even a more recent Western
ghost town. In fact, ghost towns were apt descriptions for these emptied Sudanese communities because the spirits of the one-time occupants were still
omnipresent.

These rural houses were more traditional than the ones we rented in town.
Since they were constructed of mud-plastered, sundried brick, sprawled around
enclosed open-air spaces, and contained rounded benches of mud bricks and
floors of hardened smoothed earth, they reminded us Southwesterners of home.
One noticeable difference, however, was the ornamental use of ceramic plates
plastered onto the façades. We speculated upon the possibility that they represented the various establishments in which the men worked. Not unexpectedly in this treeless tract, wooden construction details were minimal. Therefore, we were especially interested in the carved, bar-shaped, sliding wooden
door latches that contained large wooden keys. We actually removed several of
these to use as models because the boys had hit upon the idea of reproducing
them as decorative patio gate locks to sell in places such as Santa Fe. In our enthusiasm, however, we all overlooked one critical detail. It virtually never rained
in Nubia and certainly never snowed. Consequently, the wood there shrank
rather then swelled. That was not the case in Santa Fe.

The people who had been removed from the proposed basin of Lake Nasser
were permitted to take their few tangible possessions as well as a limited number of animals with them. Dogs, however, were not moved. Squads of soldiers
therefore patrolled emptied settlements to shoot these poor creatures on sight.
It was the humane thing to do under the circumstances because the beasts, left
in isolated areas from which the Nile on one side and the Nubian Desert on

Embellished country house in Nubia with resident in foreground

the other prevented escape, faced certain starvation. There had been horrid stories of such abandoned dogs attacking and eating persons who ventured into their domain. We thought about this possibility as we trespassed through the silent rooms and courtyards, but when we happened upon several new-born puppies off in a corner, our fears melted into tenderness. Nancy and Bill could not simply walk away and leave them to die. They gently picked up one little fellow and carried him back to Wadi Halfa, where he soon grew from an adorable puppy into an ugly mongrel they named Charlie. Ultimately, after going through endless red tape and long quarantines, and at great expense, they brought the dog back to the United States. Charlie, however, had so little appreciation for the good life that within a year or so, he up and died.

Dr. Louis Leakey, the African-born English archaeologist who had gained international fame through his numerous discoveries of *Homo sapiens* prede-cessors that were millions of years old, had been our house guest in Colorado during several lecture tours, and he had courteously invited us to visit his lab-oratory if we ever came to Kenya. With Ramadan approaching—a period of religious fasting and little work for our native crew—we decided to do just that. A letter from Leakey confirmed that he was at home and, moreover, that one of his sons was now operating a small safari company. We immediately signed up for a tour and took off from the same small airport where we were not allowed to step onto the sand.

On the morning that we called on Leakey in Nairobi, we just missed an earlier guest, Colonel Charles Lindbergh. To compensate for this disappointment, we were treated to a peek at the latest Leakey find—a piece of bone he called Sinjanthropus, which he had tucked into thick cotton padding and placed inside a wall compartment for safekeeping. Leakey's sponsor, the National Geographic Society, had not yet released the news of this find, but he felt that his secret would be safe with us in our Sudanese exile.

Thereafter, it was a three-week jaunt filled with memories that would last a lifetime, not the least of which was relishing all of the creature comforts and the beauties of the green and blooming landscapes that we had been missing for so long. Snow-capped Kilimanjaro, the Masai, the game animals, the archaeological sites, the sea, the Rift Valley—we gloried in them all. In the places where tourists gathered, there was still a strong adherence to English customs, since independence was only a month old. Dressing properly for dinner was one of these standards. Fresh from the field, we were wrinkled and shabby. Despite being right at the equator with its heat and extreme humidity, however, the menfolk were still expected to wear ties and jackets. That was when we realized that our youngest son had changed by several sizes over the winter in spite of our goat meat diet. His shirt collar would not button and the sleeves of his coat ended above his wrists. These were embarrassments he overcame by downing a rapid succession of lemonades and ice cream.

Back in Wadi Halfa the weather, which had been very cold in mid-winter as chilling winds swept down from Europe, turned hot again. None too soon, the projects were winding down. It was time to consolidate our notes, take final pictures and measurements, and begin packing up. Bob took time out to make a hurried train trip to Khartoum to conduct some final expedition business. To no one's surprise, the cars' wooden benches were grimy and fly-blown due to the wide-open windows. Departure for what was to be a baked, dusty ride was early. As Bob was dozing off during the midday heat, the train suddenly lurched to a halt out in the middle of nowhere. There was not a tree, a bush, a building, or even a boulder to be seen. Then, to his utter astonishment, every man, woman, and child tumbled out and unabashedly relieved himself or herself beside the tracks in what must have been the world's busiest rest stop! After these physical demands were met, the train soon once more rumbled toward its destination. This same routine was also followed during Bob's return trip.

In a few weeks we had made our last trip to the *souk*, walked by the river front to gaze out toward Gezira Dabarosa, come home through a shower of rocks, and consumed our last Camel beer. The next morning we said an aerial goodbye to Wadi Halfa and Lower Nubia as we flew back to Egypt. Confined in the rear of the plane in a box Bill had made for him, Charlie howled all the way.

We spent several days in Cairo going through the sometimes frustrating process of getting our visas for a planned two-month crossing of Asia. Our visit to the Philippine Embassy was memorable for the way in which we were warmly welcomed. It was not merely due to our own charm, but instead to the fact that the news of General Douglas MacArthur's death had just been received. MacArthur had been a great hero to the Filipinos because of his "I shall return" war exploits, and Americans in general still shared in this aura of respect and gratitude. The ambassador came to meet us personally and insisted on sending us back to our second-class hotel in his private limousine.

Needless to say, we were not treated as royally elsewhere as we embarked on a grand tour that would take us to many countries that are now so sadly off limits—Lebanon, Iraq, Iran, Afganistan, Pakistan, and Vietnam. I celebrated my birthday in New Delhi. Frank turned sixteen in Singapore, and Gary became thirteen somewhere between Tokyo and Honolulu. Bob was luckiest of all, however, since he got to celebrate his birthday back home in Colorado.

Only a few years later, Wadi Halfa, along with the eight-foot-high mounds of potsherds left in the street beside our house, disappeared beneath the river waters. Likewise gone forever were the Middle Kingdom forts, the Paleolithic petroglyphs of game animals that could not survive in modern Nubia, the windrows of hand axes, the historic sites that the Colorado group had studied, and the small airport with its ludicrous sign about keeping off the sand. It also did not take long for some of the transplanted and homesick Nubians to begin drifting back, to try and renew their lives on the desert sands.

THE SERIOUS SIDE

After returning home, it was not without some apprehension that I faced this particular pottery analysis. I had little knowledge of the regional history or of the classical archaeology from which I anticipated that these ceramics had partially been derived. Moreover, I had never worked with wheelmade, kiln-fired pottery. Luckily, I was able to draw upon the resources in our university library and upon some preliminary classificatory work of a fellow American, William Adams, who had studied some of the same problems. My own efforts were based upon visual characteristics of finished objects and upon microscopic observations of non-plastic inclusions in clay bodies. In a state of bewilderment about wheel-turned pottery processes, however, I felt the need of first-hand experience. With that goal in mind, I began pottery classes upon our return to Colorado, and I continued to be active in the craft for many years. Our yield of non-ceramic items had been very limited. My analysis of the pottery was therefore critical, not only for the temporal placement of the village site, but also for the answer to questions about social interaction and behavior.

More than 200,000 potsherds and numerous whole vessels, clay weights, bell clappers, figurines, gaming pieces, and faience had come from the digs. Pottery had been very important to what otherwise appeared to have been an impoverished society because there had been no wood or metal from which containers could be made. The pottery was both handmade and wheel-turned. Handmade vessels had likely been the efforts of informal household industries. They consisted of brown, crudely formed, thick-walled, low-fired objects that had been heavily tempered with plant materials which burned out during firing, leaving telltale channels in the clay. These vessels were not much different from the Neolithic pottery made in the same part of the world thousands of years earlier.

Wheelmade pottery, which I learned to distinguish by attributes such as throwing rings, wall and contour uniformity, and trimming marks, belonged in two broad categories. The most common pots were thick storage jars. A slender tapered amphora with a solid spiked base was particularly distinctive and surely a form that had been retained from about the beginning of the Christian Era when Rome had dominated the Nile valley. Although no physical examinations of the clay had been done, it appeared to be the same clay that had also been used by those who fashioned vessels by hand. Wheelmade decorated wares were either slipped in white or left a plain red, had some occasional naturalistic or geometric painted designs, and came in a variety of forms such as cups without handles, goblets, bowls, canteens, jars, and oil lamps. A residual classicism was apparent here, as was a generalized Egyptian influence. The range of the pottery, however, provided substantial evidence, not otherwise observable, of there having been at least three distinct cultural entities occupying the site at different periods.

The earliest inhabitants had been the Meroites, who had established their capital upriver at the Sixth Cataract and expanded northward into Lower Nubia about A.D. 100. Next had come the X-Group, a pastoral tribe for whom horses were especially important. These people had inhabited the Wadi Halfa stretch from ca. A.D. 400 to 600. Their ceramics were unusual considering their mobile lifestyle, since many pieces were almost eggshell-thin, indicating a good-quality clay resource and great proficiency on the part of the craftsmen. The homogeneity of size and style pointed to the existence of a formalized pottery industry, not just a few persons making domestic earthenwares in their yards. Finally, Coptic Christians, who were retreating from Muslimized Egypt, had filtered into Nubia about A.D. 650 and remained there for perhaps three hundred years. In the A.D. 1300s the region was then invaded by Muslims crossing the Red Sea. Some random fragments, called *ostraka,* were of particular interest because they carried painted inscriptions in demotic or ancient Egyptian, in Meriotic, and in cursive Greek scripts. Sherds from the village trash heaps had been used by literate men as convenient tablets for various notations. Had Gary not been observant, such unfired writings would have been thrown out with the wash water.

REFERENCES

Lister, Florence C. "Ceramic Studies of the Historic Periods in Ancient Nubia." *Anthropological Papers of the University of Utah,* No. 86, 119 pp., 1967.

With a Spanish Accent

During the 1950s, John Goggin, a friend from our college days, undertook an in-depth study of Spanish-tradition pottery recovered from Indian sites and galleon wrecks along the coasts of his native Florida. During the course of his work, he expanded his inquiries to include localities around the Caribbean, in Mexico, and in the Southwest where Spanish materials had been discarded from the late fifteenth through the eighteenth centuries, in the process affirming the legitimacy of extending archaeological research into the historical periods. After an auspicious beginning, Goggin died before bringing his research to full fruition.

At the time, in 1968, Bob and I were casting about for a project that we could work on together in our leisure time. We, too, had some familiarity with Spanish-style ceramics in New Mexico, and it occurred to us that we might profitably continue Goggin's work. In addition to attempting to pin down the points of derivation in Spain from which pottery had been sent overseas to Spanish colonists, we hoped to demonstrate the exported technology that led to colonial pottery-making industries.

I was confident of being able to carry out such an undertaking. From the Sudanese experience I had gained new insights into aspects of the wheel-turned pottery craft and an appreciation of studying it against a historical background. Moreover, having become a potter myself, I had acquired a tactile sensitivity that resulted from handling the revolving clay between my fingers, making the visual and mental judgments necessary to work the clay into replications of model forms, and learning the complicated chemistry of glaze formulation. I also had experienced the frustrations of unanticipated disasters caused by kiln temperatures and atmospheres.

Once we decided to proceed with this endeavor, I applied for two research grants and was turned down for both. Since sex discrimination was no longer an issue, I reasoned that academic requirements caused me to be eliminated, since I had neither an advanced degree nor an institutional connection. Thereafter, both of our names appeared on all business concerning our proposed research.

This approach was not a sham. From the beginning, we had envisioned a joint endeavor. Because we intended to base our work on extant collections and on operating workshops that might be continuing ancient technologies, Bob would contact government officials, museum directors, and shop managers in order to secure the necessary permissions for examining materials and working under their direction. He would handle logistical matters and photograph specimens, whereas I would concentrate on the pottery. At home I would research the literature and take graduate classes in Spain's political and art history. When the time came for us to report on the results of our studies, I would write the first manuscript, which Bob would then review. When required, he would prepare the line drawings and photographs, both activities in which he excelled. Whatever publications resulted would therefore truly be coauthored.

In some circles where research is driven by large sums of grant money and a cast of dozens, our private program probably would have seemed pitiful, if not mad. Few of those persons would have even considered such an undertaking that required considerable investment in time, energy, and dollars merely for personal intellectual satisfaction. Nevertheless, throughout the seventeen-year duration of our Spanish-tradition ceramic studies that took us to five continents, we almost never worked under the auspices of an academic body. This was possible because of our established credentials and because of a genuine display of cooperation by a host of colleagues scattered around the Hispanic world.

Through no solicitation by us, chemists at the Smithsonian Institution volunteered, as part of their own ongoing inquiries, to conduct comparative physical analyses of Spanish and Mexican clays. Early in the effort the American Philosophical Society and the Museum of International Folk Art each awarded us a small travel grant. The Smithsonian Institution underwrote a three-month study in Morocco. Otherwise, from our first exploratory field trip to the final book publication, it was essentially a two-person Lister endeavor. We outlined the research goals we hoped to accomplish, pursued them in accordance with the emerging questions, personally funded our own field efforts, and did our field work during accrued vacation periods from other salaried jobs. Documentary, analytical, classroom, writing, and drafting work was done in our leisure time at home. Whatever future researchers might judge to be the value of the results, for us they were educational as well as recreational, and they constituted our own small contribution to the unraveling of cultural history. Perhaps that sounds ridiculously naive, but such was the case.

Many memories of events related to our long-running Spanish ceramics research revolved around Mexico. We made excursions to Puebla, Guanajuato, Dolores Hidalgo, and Guadalajara to observe potters, so that we could acquire a feel for the rhythm and procedures of work at shops that were still connected to their European past. Generally these were disappointing for our purposes due to the infiltration of modern equipment and commercially refined materials. We sought out private and public collections of colonial pottery. Primarily we were then concerned with a type called maiolica, a tin-glazed earthenware that typified the output of Spanish decorated wares. These assortments were likewise disappointing because there was only a vague resemblance to the kind and quality of such ceramics recovered archaeologically outside of Mexico. Other than a few pieces of maiolica taken from digs on the flanks of the great pyramid at Cholula, we found that virtually no scientific excavations had been carried out in colonial sites, and local archaeologists as a body expressed total disinterest in doing so.

Soon thereafter, however, a municipal project at the capital threatened this apathy. Subway construction at Mexico City unearthed a great mass of colonial as well as Indian debris, and ethics demanded that it all be processed. So it should have been, but instead, the colonial objects were immediately put into dead storage. The speed with which our request to study the ceramics was granted underscored the feeling of official relief that the Mexican professionals would not have to trouble themselves with it. The sole exception to this rule

Modern Mexican pottery workyard with green ware air drying before firing

was a student, Gonzalo López Cervantes, who was working on a thesis topic and obviously had little choice in the matter.

The setting for our work could only be described as romantic. The colonial subway materials were tossed into huge burlap sacks and stacked in a stone-walled *bodega* behind the huge impressive Jesuit complex at Tepotzotlán, a village about twenty-five miles north of Mexico City. In the eighteenth century, the ecclesiastical installation along one side of its plaza encompassed a Baroque gilded chapel, a convent, a college, a library, some cells, and the surrounding farm lands. Abandoned during the Mexican Revolution and robbed of its portable riches, the convent was converted during modern times into a viceregal museum, and its restored chapel became a shrine for art lovers. We passed daily along their quiet corridors en route to the rear patio that was draped with vivid bougainvillea. Whether it was to watch us or the artifacts was unclear, but several assigned guards hoisted the unwieldy sherd sacks and dumped the contents out onto the ground. Then, uninterested in the proceedings, they disappeared, not to be seen again until the next morning.

With church bells loudly clanging and disturbed pigeons fluttering above,

*Sorting Spanish colonial wares from the subway excavations under Mexico City
in the patio of the former Jesuit monastery at Tepotzoltlán, Mexico*

we sat down in the patio dirt to try and sort out meaningful groupings of pottery types. Due to the Mexicans' apathetic attitudes toward historical research, their laboratory work had not included the placement of a sealant fixative over the inked provenience numbers. This omission allowed valuable information to rub off the glazed surfaces due to the friction of sherd against sherd in the storage bags. Not having access to these data, we could hope to categorize the pottery only by an analytical overview of its style. Since there were dozens of minor variations, this would not be easy or foolproof.

During our work at Tepotzotlán, we stayed in the city at the only acceptable motel, the Shirley Courts, now torn down, but for many years a landscaped sanitary Mecca for automobile travelers. We flew to Mexico City from Albuquerque and rented a car to commute to our monastic retreat. About nine o'clock on the first morning, Bob drove our rented VW bug out of the Shirley Courts right into peak traffic, and we were promptly sideswiped by a truck.

There were no passenger injuries or damage to the car, but this accident ce-
mented for us a great resolve to avoid that situation again. Thereafter we left
town at seven and returned before five, taking along a couple of sodas and
some cheese and crackers to tide us over. We paused to consume these under
a giant pepper tree. Each afternoon we smuggled a few handfuls of sherds out
of the monastery in order to work on them in the comfort of our motel room,
smuggling them back to the *bodega* the next day.

After three weeks of intensive note-taking and photographing, we packed
up a study collection to bring back home. Bob took the boxes by taxi down to
José Lorenzo's government office, which at the time was located just off the
zócalo. Lorenzo, who was head of the Instituto Nacional de Antropología e
Historia, impressed upon us the importance of what he described as a new,
strictly enforced government policy of protecting Mexico's heritage by all possible means. He carefully sealed the boxes with reams of tape that was then
stamped conspicuously with government markings about every two inches.
His secretary drafted a two-page formal letter in duplicate to the Mexican custom officials outlining our basic research and asking them to allow these artifacts to leave the country for study purposes only.

When we reached Ciudad Juárez on our return flight, the airport limousine
driver carelessly threw the sherd boxes up onto a rooftop rack. I watched their
shadows wobbling back and forth as we sped toward the Rio Grande bridge at
the border crossing, and I tried not to imagine the mad scene that would ensue,
should those boxes tumble off and split open in traffic, their precious contents
flying off in every direction and my following right after them. At the border,
the Mexican customs officer waved our limousine right on through the control
station without even glancing at the officially sealed and stamped boxes or our
packet of legal papers. Bob later wrote to thank Lorenzo, diplomatically re-
porting only that we had experienced no trouble.

One individual who enlivened our work in Mexico over a number of years
was Isabel Kelly, to me, the woman archaeologist *extraordinaire*. Bob had first
met her there in the late 1930s while traveling with Brand. He remembered
her as having once loaned him a few pesos to buy a coveted *serape* from a
street vendor. I had seen Isabel from a distance at the 1940 Chaco Conference,
but I felt that I met her more intimately a few years later. During World War II
when I worked as a Spanish translator in the Los Angeles Office of Censorship,

some of her letters from Mexico to her family in California passed over my desk. Feeling that this had been an embarrassing invasion of privacy, I thought it best never to mention these incidents to Isabel. After the war as Bob took up interrupted work in western Mexico, we saw Isabel on many social occasions, but it was during the later Spanish ceramics research that we all became good friends.

Isabel had gone to Mexico during the decade of the 1930s to conduct archaeological investigations in the western states of Colima and Sinaloa. A woman alone doing a man's work in *macho* Mexico had surely been an oddity. Village officers from whom she needed an official stamp on some paper had left her to cool her heels for hours or had openly scoffed at her ability to cope. She had endured the full gamut of field discomforts and upsets ranging from inns that were infested with bedbugs; to interminable diets of beans, rice, and tortillas; to sexual insinuations; to drunken muleteers who stole equipment. A survivor, she also was doubtlessly difficult to work with because she was demanding of herself and of her helpers. It was this concern for strict standards and detail, however, that produced such model scientific reports.

Isabel had become so enamored of Mexico's pre-Columbian past and its present that she made it her home for the ensuing fifty years and even became a Mexican citizen. One needed only to watch her drive through Mexico City's undisciplined traffic—with one foot on the accelerator, one hand on the horn, and a tongue ready to release a stream of colorful expletives in Spanish—to know that this lady had become totally acculturated.

After living around in various make-do quarters, Isabel had bought a large colonial, walled compound in the village of Tepexpán, which was located in the Valley of Mexico near the floating gardens of Xochimilco. She had the main house, several outbuildings, and the grounds converted into a lush, tranquil oasis belying the growing polluted suburbs outside. Possessing exquisite taste, she had furnished the compound with antiques she had picked up during her years in Mexico's back country, and she enjoyed a stream of visiting American scholars who came to revel in her refuge and listen to her vast anecdotal repertory about life south of the border. I particularly remember some chests that were elaborately painted and studded with brass fittings that had once held cargoes of nested Chinese porcelain teacups and rice bowls shipped on the Manila galleons from the entrepôts of the Orient to Acapulco. I also recall her large maiolica collection, about which we had numerous conversations. These often were followed by mailed references that she had found in the obscure sources she scoured during her own studies of colonial beads.

The last time we visited Isabel was when we took Hugo Nutini, a social anthropologist residing in Mexico, and several of his friends to meet her at their request. Upon seeing Isabel after several years absence, we were shocked. She had become gaunt and ashen, and she had lost tufts of her cropped iron-gray hair due to the effects of her chemotherapy treatments. Characteristically, Isabel refused to wear a wig. Characteristically, she was gracious and animated. Two years later, in 1984, Isabel Kelly died at the age of seventy-eight.

Eight years after the subway project was completed, we again returned to Mexico City to work with colonial ceramics. This haul had been produced by a massive restoration undertaking beneath and in the city's main cathedral at the heart of the Aztec and Spanish capital. We had made a preliminary visit to the enterprise the previous year and had been taken down shafts driven through the muck beneath the adjoining Sagrario to see the partially exposed façade of an Aztec pyramid that had been covered over and forgotten. This was not an uncommon find in what had been a sacred precinct of Aztec Tenochtitlán, as later work in an adjoining block confirmed. Of more direct importance to our current interests were the Spanish artifacts we watched diggers scraping out of the wet dirt.

After processing, the recovered sherds, some of which had been taken from as much as forty feet below the cathedral's floor, were eventually hoisted to the cathedral roof and then hauled on human backs to a small room in the right bell tower. An enormous bronze bell hung directly overhead, and its deafening deep boom could be heard for blocks. It was obvious to me that the deceased bell ringer who had formerly occupied this room had either had his eardrums shattered or had collapsed while merely trying to get home, because in order to reach these quarters, it was necessary to ascend the left bell tower's very steep stairway with fifteen-inch risers up an estimated height of three stories. Then one had to go up, across, and down the curved bricked exterior of the nave vault, to finally arrive, completely winded, at the room in the opposite tower. It was a tough, grimy route, but once a person had accomplished it, the location had its rewards. A vista of the oldest sector of the city was spread out below, slowly sagging into the ancient lake bed over which it had been built,

Going to work on the roof of the National Cathedral, Mexico City

but still projecting a semblance of the colonial past. In the distance during the few early morning hours before the stifling fumes of thunderous traffic had obscured them, one could see the twin peaks of Ixtaccihuatl and Popocatépetl, both towering over 17,000 feet. It was over the shoulder of Popo that some 480 years earlier, Cortez and his intrepid men had marched into this valley to change it forever, leaving behind the ceramic complex that we were studying. We liked to think that we were handling the conqueror's own dishes. Actually this was not unlikely, since his lavish palace lay directly across the street, and one of the city's main trash dumps was apparently exactly where the cathedral had been erected during the last quarter of the sixteenth century.

In addition to being a sizable collection, these finds had the added attraction of being obtained under archaeologically better conditions than those of the subway and of having their provenience data preserved. As only a relatively small assortment had been recovered from beneath the cathedral foundation laid in 1573, we were able to postulate a temporal chronology with greater confidence and incorporate some of the types found in the subway dig that had been discussed only stylistically in our earlier study. One arm of the metro subway ran in front of the cathedral at the same depth as some of the shafts that had been sunk for the restoration work. It was therefore of critical importance that almost none of the known types associated with what was then believed to be the first Mexican industry set up in the city of Puebla were among this lot of ceramics. We were thus reassured that we had solid evidence for an earlier sixteenth-century local industry that had predated the documented one at Puebla and had turned out several grades of wares to meet the needs of persons on different economic levels.

As with other facets of exported Iberian culture, we knew that Spanish pottery and its manufacturing methods had largely remained distinct from native products and practices; however, we were able to identify what may have been the first post-conquest Aztec pottery—a style of ceramic production that had attempted to infiltrate the Spanish market. This pottery was shaped and decorated according to European tastes, with the exception of an indigenous corn motif, and it was covered with a lead glaze whose formulation by the Indians may have been the result of industrial espionage. The Aztecs did not take up use of the potter's wheel, but instead, continued using their traditional hand methods of working with the same brick-red clay that had been used since the glorious days before Cortez.

As at Tepotzotlán, a guard was assigned to accompany us to the tower room where we worked. After the first day's climb and his ensuing boredom, he vanished after he had pumped a drum of water to the roof to be used for washing sherds. Except for some construction workers, we were basically left alone. We paid no attention to their activities other than being aware of their hammering and painting. On the last day of our stay, they presented us with a key to their efforts. They had built us a toilet on the roof of the national cathedral! This seemed sacrilegious, but Bob professed a desire to finally have an executive washroom. He therefore went to inspect the construction site. What he found was a whitewashed shed located behind a stone parapet, inside of which stood a white porcelain fixture that had neither connection pipes nor functioning parts.

The final day of this particular endeavor provided us with a suitable climax. Together with a few administrators, we were invited to hear a test of the newly renovated cathedral organ. The old instrument had been dismantled at astronomical cost during restoration and sent to the Netherlands for rework-ing. Now as we stood listening in the cavernous empty church, the reinstalled instrument burst forth in a glorious uplifting song that peeled up and down the aisles. Who would have thought that lowly pottery could have brought us such a thrill?

Later that same day we also experienced the darker side of Mexico. While returning from the National Museum on a crowded bus, Bob's wallet was deftly slipped from his rear pocket.

And then there was Morocco. What a beautiful, geographically varied country, with a coastal plain that enjoyed a Mediterranean climate and its flora, the snow-capped Atlas and Riff Mountains, the northern Sahara cradling a sprinkling of palm-shaded oases, and miles of unspoiled coastlines that were bordered by wide sandy beaches and craggy cliffs. The inhabitants were equally interesting and included the descendants of Arabic stock that had brought Islam to the country during the seventh century; the native Berbers, whose women still clung to their colorful dress and excessive jewelry; and the Negroid mixtures in the south, where the black and white Africas blend.

Thanks to this interesting mixture, their combined handicrafts were a delight. Thanks to the benign temperatures and fertile soil, their food was varied and good. Thanks to the long French occupation, their wines were excellent. In addition to these advantages, the Moroccan pottery craft was also known to be alive and well and had probable prior connections to that of Andalusia. Little wonder that for all of these reasons, we were excited to have the opportunity of spending three months there during the winter of 1970 thanks to the largess of the Smithsonian Institution on behalf of the American and Moroccan governments.

Morocco's history was a fascinating one. In A.D. 711 Berbers from Morocco who were led by Muslim invaders from farther east had spewed across the Straits of Gibraltar into Spain. During the next century, artisans from the Spanish Muslim capital city of Córdoba were sent into exile as punishment for plotting against their ruler. Large numbers of them moved south to Fez, the capital city of the Moroccan Muslims. There they had established a separate district called the Andalusian Quarter, where they started operating potteries. After that time the economic and social interdependence of Morocco and Andalusia had become solid, culminating in two successive Berber dynasties who seized control in Spain for about 125 years. When Christian armies drove the last of the Berbers out of Iberia in the middle of the thirteenth century, the remaining Nasrid Dynasty, which was isolated in an emirate around Granada, received constant support from their fellow Muslims across the Mediterranean for another two-and-a-half centuries. With all of this intercourse going on between these two westernmost branches of Islam, it seemed likely to us that there had probably also been a shared pattern of ceramic evolution. At least, that was what we hoped to elucidate insofar as maiolica was concerned.

In our continuous self-education process about Spanish ceramics, we stopped en route to Morocco for study at museums in London, Paris, Barcelona, Valencia, Madrid, and Lisbon. Our work routine had Bob photographing specimens while I talked into a tape recorder about what we were seeing. I felt a bit silly going about this business in galleries where other people were present, but it assured us of a more complete record.

Once at Rabat we went to meet the finance officer at the American Embassy, and he insisted on immediately giving us the full amount of our generous grant. That was a very large stack of bills in *dirhams*. We were reluctant to have to carry such a bulky sum of cash around with us, but we really had no choice. I split the lining of several zippered compartments in a roomy travel purse and stuffed the money into every bulging cranny. Thereafter, we slept each night with the purse clutched between us.

The American Cultural Affairs Officer arranged for us to meet with those top government officials and archaeologists who were mildly interested in our survey, and he provided us with an interpreter and a car and driver until we got oriented. From the Moroccans we received a packet of introductory letters to the directors of those state-controlled museums in the country which had maiolica holdings, authorizing them to facilitate our work and to permit our taking photographs. It had been our experience that such formalities were essential in Third World countries because low-level administrators, perhaps with reason, typically shied away from making such decisions on their own.

Once we had a plan of action, we rented a Renault that was just big enough for the two of us and our two suitcases. We named it Ibn Battuta after a thirteenth-century Muslim geographer from Tangiers who had wandered through the Mediterranean world. We proposed to make a series of trips to various sectors of the country, not only to see the pottery vessels and whatever relevant archaeological material there might be, but also to visit the operating workshops. We would then return from these excursions to Rabat to get our notes and thoughts in order and to pick up our mail, especially the letters from Frank and Gary who were then in college.

Our first destination was Fez, the oldest Moroccan city and still the center of a flourishing pottery activity. From the balcony of our hotel room we could look across the jumbled roofs of the original settlement's old native quarter, or *medina*. Now there are three distinct towns along and beyond the *wadi* as the population has expanded over time. A crescendo of voices, of animal hooves clattering on cobblestones, of the distant braying of donkeys, and of the high-pitched *muezzin* calls swelled up through the maze of buildings from canyon-like passageways. During the early morning we saw columns of thick black smoke rising from a concentrated spot on the opposite side of town, and we knew that the potters there had begun igniting an oily fuel of olive pressings and pits in their kiln combustion chambers.

Arrangements had been made for a veteran Arab-speaking Peace Corps volunteer to accompany us through Fez. Our first few paces down the shadowed alley into the *medina* showed us that he would have to lead us like a Seeing Eye dog, as well as make our inquiries understandable. The route ahead was a confused tangle of twists and turns along streets that were several stories deep and often only sufficiently wide for two to walk abreast. Wheeled conveyances had not been a part of Muslim culture prior to the recent historic period. For example, the creaking two- and four-wheeled *carretas,* which were used in freighting and had wheels eight to ten feet in diameter, had been a Christian contribution to Andalusian life. Wide thoroughfares were therefore not needed and would have taken up valuable space in the densely filled Muslim communities that huddled together behind towering security walls. As we moved further into the *medina*'s labyrinthine heart throbbing with animated life, we could not recognize any landmarks that might guide us out, should we ever dare to come alone. Looking around, we felt completely swallowed up.

Finally arriving at the pottery workshops, we found ourselves in the midst of an activity that seemed not to have changed for a thousand years. The air

Pottery workyard at Fez, Morocco. Kiln constructed of broken
earthenwares embedded in mud, being fired by oily olive pits and skins,
in right foreground. Donkeys carry loads of hard clay clods.

was sour and heavy with ripened clay. The open spaces between the dreary
shacks were adrift among centuries of discarded pottery rejects, known as
wasters. Untold numbers of broken pots had been poked into the mud to form
walls or to buttress the kilns. Strings of donkeys were hauling in bags of hard
clay clods or bales of fuel. Some manual workers were pounding the clay with
heavy wooden mallets in order to crush it for a preliminary sifting, and others
were stomping waist-deep in pits of clay that had already been freed of all extraneous foreign matter and moistened. Tethered beasts plodded around and
around at circular grinding pits to turn heavy flat stones over raw minerals in
order to pulverize them.

It was the potters hunched over their jobs, however, that electrified me. Their
kick wheels had been placed in trenches in the dirt floors of the dank work-
rooms, so that the wheel heads were exactly positioned at ground level. The
earth surrounding the wheels acted as work tables, with crude hand imple-
ments such as bits of shaped iron, cordage, or chamois scattered about. I had
read of such wheel-positioning in the Middle East and had assumed that it was
a practice confined to that area. Therefore, I was very surprised to find that it

was also the universal Moroccan custom, except in a few relatively recent shops where more modern, comfortable, and healthy table-high wheels had been adopted. As I watched these Moroccans throwing pot after pot in the casual manner that comes from years of practice, it suddenly struck me that pit wheels must also have been used in Muslim Spain. They had most certainly been passed on to the Christian potters who followed and then diffused to New Spain in its initial overseas pottery-making enterprises. It was a novel idea that demanded further consideration. As any researcher knows, when such a bit of stimulating information turns up, it can make one's day. I realized that we had right in front of our eyes a tableau of what the pottery industry must have been like in Andalusia before the Italians arrived in the mid-sixteenth century to make some refinements.

Otherwise, we were only able to a make few correlations between Moroccan and Spanish ceramics for the period in which we were most interested. The museum collection at Fez was an assortment of late nineteenth- and early twentieth-century pieces. It was on a par with what we had encountered in Rabat and what we would find in all of the other installations that we visited, with only one exception. At Meknes we saw half a dozen exceptionally fine conical bowls that averaged two-and-a-half feet in diameter and were of a type now used for the festive national dish of *couscous*. We were told that these bowls had been discovered locked away unused in the huge seventeenth-century palace of the Sultan Moulay Ismail. In a few other places there were some smoothed, polychrome tiles that had been a Seville specialty during the sixteenth and seventeenth centuries. Apparently most Moroccan artisans had chosen to continue using the mosaic *alicatado* style to the present. This was a tile mode that had been used most prevalently in Spain at the Nasridian Alhambra Palace and at the *mudéjar* Alcázar in Seville, buildings which were constructed during the thirteenth and fourteenth centuries. Otherwise, no maiolicas obtained through archaeological investigations were shown to us anywhere. We got the distinct impression that local scholars were not interested in pursuing such recent studies as those involving this type of ceramics.

That situation fortunately altered during the 1970s when a team from the State University of New York at Binghamton headed by Charles Redman excavated a site near Tangiers over a period of five seasons. That settlement, which had been a fortified port, could be documented as being a Muslim town from the twelfth to the fifteenth centuries. At that time it had been captured by the Portuguese and held until 1550, when it was abandoned. The recovered pottery did not clearly fall into Muslim and Christian categories due to the conservative continuum of the craft, but simple domestic wares covered with a thin white glaze typified the Portuguese occupation. Happily for our research, it was identical to that which had been identified as late fifteenth- and early sixteenth-century Seville ceramics and that which was known to have come from the Caribbean outposts that were established during the first fifty years of the opening of the Americas. Coinage and archival materials helped to give some of this pottery what it had lacked thus far in Andalusia—a specific niche in the calendar.

We were not so myopic in our concentration on maiolica ceramics that we ignored other kinds of pottery as we traveled around Morocco. It was an integral part of the material paraphernalia of life there and no doubt always had been. This applied to the rural Berbers even more than to the urbanized Arab component of the society, who had greater opportunity and resources for acquiring modern plastic containers and butane cook stoves. Earthenware in one form or another has always been used for every conceivable purpose, from feeding the chickens to preparing and serving the ubiquitous mint tea. Although some wheel industries have now begun to decorate lead-glazed wares by painting them with small-scale Berber textile patterns executed in mineral oxides, those vessels that were most characteristic were handmade and often bore designs applied in liquid pitch. Scholars have speculated that the importance of pottery in Spain stemmed from the fact that it was often a treeless environment that made wooden utensils almost non-existent. This was also the case in the Middle East, where the Spanish Muslims had originated, and perhaps to some extent, it was also true in old Morocco, since many of the trees that now mantle the valleys and slopes there are more recently introduced varieties, such as the eucalyptus.

One day's journey out from Rabat took us through rolling vineyards, over the snowy Middle Atlas Mountains, and down onto the sere northern Sahara. We headed for Erfoud, which is the trade center for much of the southeastern part of Morocco that is cut off beyond the mountains and also the site of Sijilmassa. This city had once been a thriving metropolis located at the terminus of an important caravan route stretching north from Timbuktu, over which the gold that sustained the Berber rulers in Spain was transported. It was sacked during the middle of the seventeenth century and never fully recovered its glory. Due to the region's extreme dryness, many of its rammed earthen house walls had remained standing for over three hundred years as jagged monoliths, which were two and three stories high and were banked by gigantic drifts of sand. Sijilmassa's history had been documented for many centuries before its demise and therefore promised to be a potential source of information showing some kind of ceramic linkage to Andalusia. When one of our Southwestern colleagues, Robert Euler, who was then in the process of applying for a research grant in order to test the site, had asked us to serve as the ceramic consultants for the project, we naturally jumped at the chance. Hoping to participate in the effort, we went to look over the locale. Before we left Morocco, however, we regretfully learned that his proposal had been denied and with it, our ceramic opportunity.

As in the Sudan, the Moroccan children were also often an annoyance. It seemed that no matter how remote the locality might be, we would no sooner stop Ibn Battuta to eat our lunch or get out our camera, than one or more youngsters would come over the hill, shout "Bon jour," and then stand around to watch our every move or beg to serve as our guides. Thankfully, however, they had not yet taken up the rock-throwing habit. By using sign language at Sijilmassa, Bob put the usual motley troupe to work scouring the surface for potsherds. The urchins were moderately successful, handing us pocketfuls of fragments whose surfaces had been sandblasted over the years, but whose designs and colors still had some amorphous similarities to the Andalusian pottery types. When it came time for us to leave, Bob discovered that he had only one large coin. He gave this to the apparent ringleader, gesturing to the boy that it should be equally divided among all. The boy nodded in agreement, but as we drove off, we saw the group engaged in a rough free-for-all over ownership rights.

It was market day at the neighboring village of Rissani. Piles of unglazed red cooking and storage pots in several shapes and sizes were stacked on the ground for sale. We watched others being unloaded from a netting laced over a camel's back. Some of the clay objects that had served the populace since the Roman days were cooking devices. These were unfired greenware braziers that consisted of a squat pedestal base topped with a bowl-shaped unit containing basal

Prospective purchaser examines a Moroccan amphora whose shape goes back centuries to Roman prototypes but is made through a combination of techniques. The base is hand formed and trimmed, with upper shoulder and neck being fashioned on a pit wheel.

Camels taking pots to market in Morocco

Earthenware braziers for sale at Moroccan market. Hot coals are placed in bottom, with cook pots resting on three-pronged supports above.

air holes in which lumps of charcoal would rest. Presumably it was intended that the users' cooking fires would harden the braziers for durability. Several such stoves were being used around the market area, as women prepared hot food to sell.

A boy of about ten or twelve years of age approached us with the customary "bon jour, want a guide" greeting. Seeing that he understood some English, Bob asked if there were any potters working in the vicinity. His answer was yes, but he said that we would have to drive ten miles or so to get there. The boy then went with us to show us the way to what turned out to be a monumental, two-story, flat-topped, blocky structure that had no exterior windows but instead, had spaced drains for the waste water that was coursing down on the outside and a single massive doorway. Tilled fields greening with new spring crops spread away from this isolated *casbah*, but there was no sign of anyone working them.

Through the portal we followed right behind our erstwhile leader and suddenly found ourselves being thrust back into a time warp. It was almost like reliving the Middle Ages. The overpowering piercing odors of stale air, cooked foods, and long-utilized latrines engulfed us. We wound our way through a congestion of open galleries—long dark hallways leading to cellular rooms where people seemed to be watching us out of the shadows—past open courts that served as playgrounds for half-naked toddlers, mangy dogs, and bleating goats; up short flights of steps and then down again; through low doorways; and past a well, where a woman was drawing water to fill a large, two-handled pottery jar. Judging by this boy's mental map of the place, I was certain that he was a resident there, because I thought that a stranger would surely have had to ask for directions. Thoroughly confused about how we had accomplished this feat, we came out onto a second-story porch overlooking a large patio. Sure enough, down below four or five men were engaged in the various processes of making pottery. Several were seated at pit wheels throwing vessels like those we had seen at the village market. They smiled and nodded for us to come closer. Details of the arrangements varied, but in general, this was a way of working that we had by then also witnessed in other places. Partly to be gracious and partly because it was an exotic background, Bob snapped a number of pictures while the men self-consciously performed, like actors on a stage.

In an aside, I asked Bob about tipping. He told me that it would be improper, since these were craftsmen who took pride in their skills and would be offended by such an offer. As we turned to go, however, no one needed to tell him that he had made a very erroneous judgment. The mood soon turned ugly as the men crowded around our little guide, shouting, gesticulating, and casting dark menacing glances in our direction. Getting the message very quickly, Bob dug out some *dirhams,* which he passed around to the sullen, still-grumbling recipients. Very uneasy and with a pounding heart, I stepped back to the doorway, realizing that I did not have the faintest idea of how we had arrived at this patio. The boy pushed in front and again led us on the circuitous route to the *casbah*'s single exit.

Outside again in the clean fresh air, we were limp with relief, realizing that in our innocence, we, along with our camera, recorder, watches, rings, and ever-present money bag, could have vanished inside that *casbah* without a trace. Bob gruffly said, "*Your* (get that!) pottery work gets us in the damnedest predicaments!"

Our next destination was Teneghir, another desert oasis that was located west across open country on a paved, but seldom-used road. We had planned to buy gas for Ibn Battuta at the midway dot on the map, but when we got there, no gas was available. The gauge was on the red; so we did the natural thing—we drove faster. At Teneghir there was also no gas. We tried to put that out of our minds as we checked into a new, government-run inn that had been built to encourage tourism.

This edifice was constructed in the regional architectural style—a rammed earthen block that was the same color as the surrounding cliffs. The very thick walls and latticed wooden blinds made it a cool shelter from the desert heat and glare. Our room window looked straight toward the mud-colored, ruined hulk of what might have been a former French Foreign Legion outpost or an abandoned *medina*. We would not have been surprised to see Ronald Coleman or some other cinema hero from our youth come charging out of the great wooden iron-studded gate in full Legionnaire's regalia. The village itself looked like a picture in *National Geographic,* with its large communal houses stacked against the rocky ridge so that its inhabitants could watch over the palm-ringed gardens that had been brought to life by water and sunshine.

That evening as we left the hotel dining room, the desk clerk stopped us to say that a man who was sitting in the small lobby enjoying a demitasse wished to speak to us. After exchanging introductions, we learned that he was an American from Chicago who was on an extended stay in Morocco. Apparently lonely, he came to the hotel several evenings each week to talk to any of his countrymen who might be passing through. He told us that he had been a tourist here himself some years earlier and had become so fond of his boy guide during his travels that he had informally adopted him and taken him back to the States to be educated. Periodically he brought his charge back for a visit with his biological family. And who was this benefactor giving a Muslim a chance? A Jew. When he heard our reasons for being in Morocco, he insisted that we go with him the next day to a village where the boy's uncle was a *marabout,* or holy man, and where making pots was a leading activity. We planned to meet the next morning.

Back in our room, I went into the bathroom to shower before retiring. Absentmindedly, I turned the lock. A few minutes later when I tried to open the door, the lock was jammed. I banged and tugged to no avail. Bob jimmied and swore from the other side with the same negative results. The bath was an interior room with no windows and no vent. Besides knowing that I was going to suffocate, I also knew that I was going to do it in pitch darkness, since the generator for the lights would cut off promptly at ten, only a few minutes away. Frantically Bob rushed down to the office to try and rouse some English-speaking help, but he had little hopes of doing so because the place closed down tightly as soon as the last of the dinner guests had departed. I slumped down to wait, every few seconds working the knob in hopes of jarring the stubborn lock loose. This situation was embarrassing, not to mention potentially dangerous. It was also funny, but I was not yet ready to laugh. Finally, I heard voices that were loud enough to ensure that everyone in our hotel wing would know of the predicament in which the American woman in Room 20 found herself. The debate raged on. Should they try to find tools to remove the door from its hinges, should they smash it in, or should they perhaps cut a hole through the two-foot thick wall? Meanwhile, someone slipped a knife blade between the door and the latch, and the lock tumbler fell. The door opened just as the lights went off. I did not die of mortification in a toilet in Teneghir.

Al Hart, the home of the *marabout,* was a verdant and peaceful vision of desert beauty. In the twentieth century it was also an island of unreality characterized by desolation, oppressive customs, and abject poverty. Its women were hidden behind burdensome black draping that permitted only a single eye to be exposed. Lacking sufficient residents for a *casbah* or *ksar,* its single houses had no electricity, liquid gas, or running water. Its small fields depended upon an ancient, squeaking wooden wheel with a chain of pots that raised precious water from a deep well and dumped it into the tiny irrigation canals. By sharing in their sacrifices, the village occupants entirely supported the special man we were to meet.

Our old host, with an appropriately wizened, saintly appearance, ushered us into a reception room that was devoid of furnishings except for several of the country's knotted rugs. We sat down on these carpets, while a barefoot youth brought in a tea tray that was dominated by a large brass bowl that stood on legs and had a conical lid. This was the customary container for the lumps of coarsely refined sugar that Moroccans use lavishly in their tea and that must account for the many snaggle-toothed mouths seen throughout the country. While the Jew and the Muslim politely conversed in Arabic, we took in the simple surroundings that seemed familiar to us Southwesterners. A single, deep-set window that pierced a massive hand-plastered wall and still showed visible fingerprints opened to a clump of date palms.

Our formalities over, we walked across an opening between the houses to a yard where two male potters were at work forming handmade vessels. They slammed a patty of moist clay over a large, cone-shaped rock and hastily tapped it with a mallet until the clay had thinned and expanded around the natural mold. The edge was then trimmed and compacted to form a rim. Finally, a bunch of wet grass was wiped over the surface, and after a matter of three or four minutes, the pot was finished. As had been done for ages, such vessels were then fired in a shallow depression in the ground that was heaped over with fronds and brush to serve as fuel. This was the most rudimentary production level that we observed in Morocco. It was quite in keeping with the cultural status of Al Hart, which had a thin veneer of the Islamic sphere's civilizing forces, but which at heart remained natively tribal.

After our visit to Al Hart, we returned to our headquarters in Rabat to analyze and collate the information we had gathered during our trip. Driving back, we were glad to see that the gas truck had fortunately reached the way station we had passed en route, and we could once again fill Ibn Battuta's empty stomach.

One of our lengthiest treks from Rabat took us almost to the southern Moroccan border to Goulemime, where a tribe of blue-robed men brought camels to a famed market. We stayed at an exceedingly primitive hotel with odorous communal facilities and watched a program of discordant falsetto singing and ceremonial belly dancing by corpulent, jewelry-bedecked ladies whose contractions produced great rolling waves of flesh that resembled breakers rushing in to shore. The village was filled with troops of disheveled hippies bargaining for trinkets. Views from our room of a sea of ungainly camels and their keepers remain unforgettable memories.

In the course of this trip we visited Safi, begun as one of the series of forts built in the fifteenth century by the Portuguese as they moved down the western coast of Africa eventually reaching the Cape of Good Hope. Nowadays a modern industry at Safi turns out maiolica bearing dense geometrical patterns of mechanical precision. The table-high kick wheels, whitewashed kilns, and spic-and-span salesrooms there held little inteest for us. We made use of some homesick Peace Corps volunteers as interpreters and spent an evening with

Moroccan country potter working on pit wheel. Round bottomed vessels at left, formed over a rock mold, waiting to be finished off on the wheel

them listening to the problems they were experiencing as instructors in the local elementary schools. At Marrakesh we observed the Almohad minaret, which resembles the one that looms over the Seville skyline; photographed a large collection of ceramics in the museum; and wandered through the extensive bazaar where storytellers, fire-eaters, and snake charmers attracted an interested audience. It was at Essaouira on the coast during a prolonged period of feasting, however, that we finally determined the purpose of the hourglass-shaped earthenware we had watched being made and decorated at Fez and at other locations. They were small ceramic drums, each head covered with a thin wet hide that contracted into place as it dried. It seemed that everyone there had such a drum, which they slapped incessantly with the palms of the hands. People formed impromptu circles along the streets of the town, and the constant throbbing of their drums and the chanting that accompanied it produced a mass hypnosis. One man whom we watched collapsed in a trance, his pottery drum shattering as he fell.

When we got ready to leave Morocco, the embassy boxed up the specimens

*Green ware about to be fired without the benefit of a formal kiln
at a Moroccan village work area*

we had purchased for the Museum of International Folk Art. They also provided us with letters of explanation in French for the Moroccan customs, in Spanish for the officers in Madrid where we had to change planes, and in English for the Americans at JFK in New York. We breezed through Casablanca and Madrid with our three large cartons unopened, but we were worried that in New York, we would have to unpack. We arrived there at a peak time, and the agents were tired and harassed. Worse yet, the one checking our luggage got into a heated argument with the woman in front of us. It was certain he was also going to give us a hard time. When Bob handed him our embassy letter, he glanced at it and threw it back at us. "I can't read that damned thing," he stormed. By mistake Bob had pulled out the letter in French. Knowing that we were then probably doomed to a long delay, Bob began to explain that we had been working abroad under the auspices of the Smithsonian Institution. That was as far as he got. Apparently, he had uttered the magic words—Smithsonian Institution—because we were abruptly waved through the line, our three boxes untouched.

The overseas diffusion of Spanish ceramics to Mexico, the beginnings of a provincial industry based upon Hispanic methods, and the resultant spread of that central Mexican pottery to the northern borderlands were only pieces of the greater puzzle about the transfer of wares and manufacturing techniques to other sections of the colonial world. Moreover, we felt that recovered ceramics could be used in a very practical way to plot some of the social and economic interactions that prevailed at different times in colonial Spanish America. To try and fill in these gaps in our background knowledge, we obtained help from the American Philosophical Society to arrange a six-week reconnaissance trip through the Caribbean and into western South America.

Our first stop in this junket was Santo Domingo, capital of the Dominican Republic. We were met at the airport by a museum official, not in the lounge as was customary, but at the stairs leading down from the plane. This seemed surprising, since we had not yet cleared customs. Without being given an explanation, we were whisked into the VIP lounge where someone thrust small cups of black coffee at us. Then as the TV cameras moved in, we were asked to comment first on the coffee and then on the great role that the Dominican Republic had played in the history of the Hispanic world. Unprepared, our answers must have come across as stammering. In retrospect, we decided that the reason behind this unexpected attention was that we had set up our appointments using Bob's official letterhead that included his title of Chief Archeologist for the U.S. National Park Service. Actually his job and our private research were unrelated, but his government connections seemed to carry a weight that we accepted with gratitude.

Early the next morning we were picked up at our hotel by Elpidio Ortega, the museum staff member who had met us at the airport, his wife, and José Cruxent, an eminent Venezuelan archaeologist also working with maiolica, for an all-day drive across the island of colonial Hispaniola. Ortega, as we soon learned, was a prime candidate for hypertension. He floorboarded the car all the way, with animals and people scurrying to get off the narrow road as we zoomed by. This driving routine was broken every forty-five minutes or so by a snack stop. Elpidio allowed us to only partially consume some sweet or drink before he took off again at breakneck speed.

The featured attraction of this field trip was Isabela, the remains of the first European town in the New World, established in January 1493 by Columbus after his second outbound voyage. The ruin's locale was a low-lying bench above the sea on Hispaniola's northern coast. It was an unfortunate choice, since the harbor was poor and lay in a hurricane path. The twelve hundred or more colonists that Columbus had brought with him had no intention of settling down there to make new homes as long as there was any hope of obtaining quick wealth by robbing the natives or by mining. They also died rapidly from disease, from their unaccustomed exertion under tropical conditions, and from strife among themselves or with those they sought to subjugate. The settlement that consisted of a few stone buildings for the leaders and thatch huts for the followers was vacated within four years to become just another testimonial to unfulfilled dreams. Two or three limited excavation efforts demonstrated that this short period was long enough for America's first non-Indian ceramic litter to accumulate. The huts quickly rotted in the humidity, but evidence of decayed masonry structures could still be seen during the last century. Slowly, however, these remains crumbled off into the same ocean through which Columbus had charted his first voyage.

Today shanties of peasants encroach upon the site. Rumor has it that a city slicker pays the simple dwellers there to pothunt the premises for its relics. Bob was aghast at the official disinterest shown in protecting this historical spot. At the time it did not boast even a sign to inform the public of its significance, and the roads leading to it were not maintained.

I strolled across the grassy surface where the old community had briefly stood half a millennium earlier and paused under a large tree that had taken root in the remains of a foundation. As I looked out over the placid bay, I tried to reach across the chasm of time and sense the Admiral's feelings about the rare combination of fates that had brought him to this very place, and just as quickly, had driven him away. As a memento, Elpidio brought me a terra cotta tile fragment that Bob had taken from an embankment. Turning it over in my hand, I thought to myself that if we had already dealt with Cortez's dishes, why not also deal with Columbus's roofing? These idle musings did not detract

me from the hard archaeological facts, since the Iberian elite and the common-
ers democratically shared the same ceramic material things. One had to admit,
however, that they injected an appealing personalization into the study's brew.

The recovered ceramics from Isabela consisted of utilitarian storage vessels
that had been used to ship supplies from Spain and a few basic cooking and
serving utensils. They were exactly like those that had been found in early
Spanish remains in Cuba, Puerto Rico, and Jamaica in the northern Caribbean;
in Venezuela and Panama in the south; and in Florida, where they represented
shipwreck rather than occupational debris.

In Santo Domingo the government had initiated an important restoration
of much of the colonial quarter, and a great volume of pottery was being retrieved from the church and domestic structures. Some was found to have been
incorporated into the fill over vaulting and beneath floors. These were discarded jars in which foodstuffs had been kept; earthenware that had been utilized in refining the sugar that became a leading export; and broken dishes,
drinking bowls, and cooking pots. The use of pottery in the fabric of buildings
had been a common practice in Spain dating from the Roman era. It was introduced to Santo Domingo by masons known to have been brought there
from Seville. The collection of these and other ceramics found in the old city
and thought to date from the early sixteenth into the early nineteenth centuries differed from others we had seen in the Americas by its inclusion of
many European examples other than those identified as being Spanish or Italian. This was concrete evidence that an extensive contraband trade had existed throughout the West Indies, which smuggled in English, Dutch, French,
and German wares despite official sanctions against the import of non-Spanish
products. We were given a small sample of the Spanish types for study purposes.

In Panama a group of amateur archaeologists led by Edwin Webster, an
Episcopalian rector from the Canal Zone, showed us assortments of sherds
they had gathered from the ruins of Spanish *rancherías* and from way stations
located along the trails across the Isthmus. Some of these occupational areas
are now seasonally covered by waters that have backed up from the Canal and
its locks. Most of this pottery was identical to the early types that we had seen
in the Dominican Republic and considered to be from Spain. There was also a
second grouping of ceramics that we learned had likely come from workshops

that had been set up in the first settlement established on the American west coast, now known as Panama Viejo.

Panama Viejo was destroyed in the 1670s by Henry Morgan, the English pirate who ravaged much of the Caribbean basin. A number of years prior to our visit, a nearby kiln had been uncovered and eradicated by a road crew. The associated pottery wasters that regional archaeologists rushed to save showed that local wares had been made of a distinctive red clay and often were decorated with a thick, white, opacified tin glaze that was covered by blue, green, and brown decorations. These potters had shared a common technical background with their probable contemporaries who worked in the late sixteenth-century pottery-making activity in Mexico City. A differing stylistic mode suggested that Panamanian potters had drawn upon another Hispanic resource for inspiration. The government workers who had explored Panama Viejo allowed us to select a random sample of the locally made maiolicas.

Moving on to the south, we contacted Father Parras, a Catholic priest in Quito who had directed some students in test excavations in the gardens of the enormous San Francisco monastery there. This edifice on the main plaza had been built during the early colonial fervor to bring Indian converts into the fold, and it had remained an active institution during subsequent centuries. The unearthed fragments the priest displayed to us were of the types we had just viewed in Panama Viejo. Previously this same gentleman had asked us to examine a collection of potsherds from excavations that he, Clifford Evans, and Betty Meggars, both employees of the U.S. National Museum, had recovered during their work on an interior Ecuadorian Amazon drainage project. We obtained a sample study assortment and tentatively identified that pottery as also being Panamanian, thereby confirming that a previously unsuspected late sixteenth- or early seventeenth-century traffic in pottery from Panama to the south had indeed taken place.

Also in Quito, another priest led Bob up onto the roof of a chapel in the Santo Domingo church to show him some tiles that had been secured to the dome. Quite unlike the Panamanian pottery, these tiles were green and were decorated with crudely painted yellow and brown patterns. We theorized that they were probably the result of some local, low-level potting activity and not particularly old.

In Lima, finds of pottery in outlying house mounds that had been made by a professor and her students from the Catholic University showed us that during the late sixteenth century, objects from the Panamanian shops had also traveled down the western coast of South America at least as far as the capital of the Viceroyalty of Peru. That trade had not been previously reported. This was not surprising, however, because Panama Viejo was not only the main market on the long sea and land route between Lima and Seville, but it was also the source for other commodities needed in the south.

Because digging had not been conducted in the right places, none of the wares from the early Spanish complex had been found in Peru. One must assume that early arrivals in Peru had brought with them their customary items for daily life; however, a flourishing market for late sixteenth- and early seventeenth-century Seville polychrome tiles is known to have existed in Lima. It is now difficult to determine which of the extant examples are the originals and which are the copies that were made after one of the numerous earthquakes brought the colonial buildings tumbling down. The same green pottery with brown and yellow designs that we had seen in Quito's rooftop tiles could also be observed in a private collection to which the American Cultural Affairs Officer directed us. In Cuzco we used Bob's pocketknife to pry comparable fragments from consolidated deposits that banked some streets. We suspected that the sherds and completely green vessels had been a body of work by artisans who lacked high standards and urban influences and who had turned out only simple wares for the mountain villagers.

Returning to the north again, we were introduced in Guatemala to the director of the National Museum, Luis Lújan Muñoz. In his official capacity, he had secured examples of colonial maiolica from Antigua, formerly known as Santiago de los Caballeros, and was himself a collector. He allowed us to examine and photograph these objects and then graciously drove us out to Antigua to visit colonial monuments and the currently operating pottery workshop. The quality and styles of the local output had altered so little for an estimated three hundred years that even the experts could not positively separate the old from the new. Because of insufficient exploration, the early Spanish complex had not been noted there.

In a later trip to Antigua by public bus, we called upon Ed and Virginia Shook, whom we were told had amassed an important collection of pottery during the restoration of a colonial home. Ed, a Carnegie Institution archaeologist who had specialized in the ancient Maya and whom Bob had met many years earlier at Harvard, had purchased a part of what had been the Santo Domingo monastery, which was destroyed in the frightful late eighteenth-century earthquakes that completely devastated the town. He and his wife had dug through the rubble exactly as they would have examined a Mayan mound and were currently in the process of having a contemporary house erected within the remains of the old stone walls. They had uncovered one of the friars' *bodegas,* which was filled to the roof with the remains of service and storage receptacles and dishes, medicine jars, and urinals that all bore a hastily applied escutcheon of the Order. Judging by the clay, the decorations, and the caliber of workmanship, we decided that these had probably originated in a local shop. In many respects they varied only slightly from what was then for sale at the current outlets. Fragmentary examples of the types that had been made in seventeenth- and eighteenth-century Puebla, however, revealed that a limited trade from the north had existed in spite of Antigua's isolated location deep in the beautiful Guatemalan highlands. Somewhat less important was the ceramic commerce coming from the Guatemalan Caribbean coast that accounted for the presence of a few tiles from Seville and some ceramic wares from Italy. Undoubtedly, earthenware jugs full of Andalusian wine likewise had been carted up from the coast. They are now used as ornamental accents in patio gardens.

The Shooks gave us a large sample of the various types from their *hacienda* that, when added to the other sherds we had already gathered throughout the trip, completely filled my carry-on cosmetic case. When the customs agent in Texas opened this bag and saw the shattered pottery, he looked at me sympathetically and said, "Lady, did you have an accident?" Bob quickly responded with a simple "no," as we walked away. Experience had already taught us the first rule of international travel, which was never to volunteer information to a customs official.

Five years after our initial trip to the Caribbean, we felt that we needed to further improve our first-hand knowledge of the kinds of pottery that had been reclaimed in the former Spanish islands. We had not visited some key places, and publication of the limited work that had been accomplished there either had never been completed or was long overdue.

A case in point was Cuba. Throughout the colonial period, Havana had been an obligatory stop for all vessels returning to Spain. This meant that a cross-section of material goods surely would have found its way into the trash heaps there. Restoration work was underway in the old quarter of the city, but we could only learn of the recovered ceramics by going there. Unfortunately, however, we were thwarted in our efforts to obtain visas.

Nevertheless, we still had other places where we could go to examine collections that we felt would give us a satisfactory overview. Beginning with St. Augustine, Florida, we planned to make a month-long swing through Jamaica, Haiti, the Dominican Republic, and Puerto Rico; and we arranged our meetings accordingly.

In all of our knocking about the world in remote places, we had never felt threatened except for that one brief episode in Morocco. But by the late 1970s we were older, and the tenor of the times had changed. Our home in New Mexico had been burglarized, leaving psychological scars that the insurance could not ameliorate, and the daily news seemed composed primarily of accounts of a national crime wave. Therefore, for reasons we could not exactly pinpoint, we felt some apprehension about going on this trip. When Bob explained that he was going to carry an empty dummy wallet in his rear pocket while putting most of his large bills in an inner zippered compartment in his leather belt, however, I thought he was being a bit paranoid. Soon the same sense of uneasiness caught up with me while we were waiting for a plane connection in Miami. I sat looking at my heirloom diamond rings and wondered why I had been foolish enough to wear them. I had not been without them for thirty years, but at that moment I wished that I had left them behind in our safety deposit box. Going into an airport shop, I bought a pack of safety pins, just in case I decided to hide my rings later on.

We flew from Miami to Kingston, but unfortunately, our luggage did not. The airlines clerk assured us that the bags would be on the next flight two hours later. He then advised us to go to our hotel and told us that he would see our suitcases through customs and send them on to us by taxi. That meant leaving him our keys. Reluctantly, we agreed, telling each other that we had to trust someone.

The taxi ride to the hotel, which turned out to be on a hill on the far side of the city, took us through miserable slums where piles of garbage lay rotting on the streets. Dogs and children were playing in the midst of this filth. The hotel was advertised as being a government-run model training school for hotel management. From its seedy, soiled appearance and the indifferent attitude of its help, it was obvious that the school was not a rousing success. The missing luggage and all of these negative first impressions were unsettling. I decided to pin my rings to my underwear. Bob called the airport several times as the afternoon progressed to check on our suitcases. No one answered the phone. It was Saturday. The clerk had gone home early.

Things began to look better the next morning when our bags arrived. Bob made the taxi driver wait while we checked them on the lobby floor. Everything was intact. Relieved to have this problem behind us, we walked to the street in front of the hotel and flagged down the city bus. It was a rattletrap affair, filled with blacks who moved over to give us a seat. We were bound for the center of town and planned to locate the museum, where we had an appointment the next morning. We rode to the end of the bus line and found ourselves in an old district made up of the architecture that was typical for hot climates—weather-beaten frame buildings with wide sheltering roofs out over the sidewalks. At the time we did not think it strange that there was not a white person anywhere in sight.

Not finding the museum street, Bob stopped a passing pedestrian to ask for directions. The waylaid man said that he was a constable and under other circumstances, he would have been happy to guide us there. Now, however, it was his day off and he had to meet a friend. As we turned in the direction that he had pointed, we soon had reason to wish for his presence. We passed a church whose door was open. The Sunday morning service was under way, and we could hear the congregation singing and saying loud amens. A black youth got up off the front steps and moved in behind us. A block down the street, he was still there. We walked faster. So did he. Hoping to rid ourselves of him, we veered to cross the empty street.

At that point the young man sprang in front and began sparring with Bob and kicking at him like a Thai boxer. Stunned at this totally unexpected situation, I yelled for help. Some figures were silhouetted against the horizon as they stood down by the bay. They turned at my cries, and four young blacks came flying toward us. Instinctively I realized I should never have called to them. They were like jackals descending on an embattled prey. One fellow leaped at me and knocked me to the pavement. My sunglasses went flying off, but not completely being off guard, I fell on my shoulder handbag. My assailant was right on top of me as we squirmed around on the street, tugging and kicking. By this time, Bob had also been downed. Struggling to free himself, he almost had my purse in his grasp when the gang broke it from my shoulder and dashed off.

For a few moments we just lay there, wondering what terror had struck us on this bright Sunday morning. Then very soon we had to face the hard fact that our plane tickets, traveler's checks, passports, eyeglasses, and many of our other personal effects were gone. Our clothes had been ripped and smeared with pavement grease. Bob had a large welt rising on his forehead. My knees were bleeding, and my upper arm and shoulder already were swelling and turning black. It was not until we got on our feet that Bob realized that his watch had been slipped from his wrist. It was even later still that we thankfully remembered the money safe in Bob's belt and the rings fastened to my underwear.

That long afternoon was spent at the pitiful excuse for a police station and at the American Embassy. In both places we were assured that we had been lucky not to have been knifed. That was small consolation. We had walked right into a war zone, where two days earlier there had been a fierce riot, during which buses were overturned and people killed. Whites had been warned to stay away from this area and not to ride the buses.

After taking down our statements, a consular official took us back to our hotel. As we entered the lobby, two men in civilian clothes approached us, said they were police, and handed us a manila envelope containing many of our stolen articles. Not surprisingly, that did not include our plane tickets or the $1200 in traveler's checks. They refused to tell us how they happened to have found our things. Bob's doubts about their legitimacy increased when shortly thereafter the embassy man called to tell us that upon leaving our hotel, he had been accosted by the same men. They had asked him many questions about us and our plans, and he had reason to think that they might try to lure us away on some pretext and force us to sign the checks. Or rather, force me, since the checks were issued in my name. He advised us to stay in our room and not to answer the door. He would come for us in the morning in a bullet-proof embassy car! After that scary conversation, we lay awake all night behind barricaded doors.

Although we spent most of the next day in the comforting protection of the embassy, we canceled our plans for continuing the trip. Our zest for pottery had dissipated. A courier was sent to get us new tickets. The museum director came by to pick up the books that we had brought at her request. The consular officer walked us to the bank to report the loss of our checks, escorted us to lunch, and finally put us in the car of a trusted employee to go to the airport. There, we took time to buy a souvenir bottle of Jamaican rum. Once we reached U.S. soil and were snugly resettled, we sat down and consumed it all. Bob was right. My pottery studies did get us into the damnedest predicaments!

Two years later the consular official who had befriended us in Jamaica and whose name I no longer remember was among the fifty-three hostages seized at the American Embassy in Tehran. After that ordeal, he safely retired to Sun City, Arizona.

When we began our maiolica studies, the role the Italians had played in Andalusian ceramics was not yet fully appreciated. Potters familiar with some Italian stylistic modes, for example those of Urbino, had been credited with stimulating and directing what later became the most popular Spanish industry at Talavera de la Reina. Their technological introductions, however, had been ignored. Any such comparable Italianization at Seville, other than in tile decoration, could not be recognized. Goggin suggested a possible design influence but did not further explore the matter. Nor would he likely have been successful had he done so. Italian archaeologists were as late in beginning the study of medieval horizons as were the Americans and the Spaniards. Only during the late 1960s and early 1970s did scientists begin studying the Italian potting centers that had operated during this time and yielded an output that had a direct impact upon southern Spanish commerce and artisanship.

After we had published a brief article on our finds from the Mexico City subway, a man from Milan wrote to warn us that we should be alert to the possibility that intrusive Italian ceramics had reached colonial New Spain. According to him, some of the published pictures of Mexican pottery recalled post-medieval Italian types. Furthermore, in some of his own independent research, he had detected Italian surnames in the Puebla guild records. To substantiate his premise, he followed up this correspondence by sending us reprints of Italian ceramic articles that were not available in this country.

The most frequently involved style that was recovered in Mexico and the Caribbean and suggested an Italian source was a very thin, finely made ware covered with a soft blue glaze, over which were placed delicate, carefully drafted arabesques in a darker blue. I was excited to learn that excavations of a kiln and other sites had identified this pottery as being the stock-in-trade for potteries in the Genoa area during a fifty-year period that corresponded to the second half of the sixteenth century. In a heartwarming display of the universal thirst for knowledge, it was only through the interest and thoughtfulness of this fellow ceramist, Guido Fowst, who lived in another part of the world, that we were made aware of this aspect of the problem.

The questions of why and how such pottery got from Genoa to Seville and then to the Americas launched me into lengthy historical research. It opened my eyes to the fact that the Genoese, among all of the other foreigners who had been attracted to the important Andalusian port, had played a particularly prominent role in Seville's life, beginning with the thirteenth-century recapture of the city from the Muslims and lasting through its sixteenth-century overseas colonization. Whereas other Europeans had been excluded from any participation in the American adventure, the Genoese were granted special privileges because they financially underwrote many of the ventures. Aggressively business-oriented while the Spaniards were not, they saw to it that specialties of their brethren, such as earthenware, got channeled into the new overseas markets to compete with and in some instances, to replace Iberian merchandise. Merely by studying these recovered ceramics, one might be able to gain insight into the otherwise obscured, but contorted political and economic undertow of the Hispanic colonial world. That analysis in itself was a long way from the mere temporal alignment of my beginning efforts in ceramic studies.

To be certain that this pottery was properly identified, we accepted an invitation in the fall of 1978 to attend a ceramic conference in the Ligurian area of northwestern Italy. Taking sherds that had been recovered from beneath Mexico City and photographs of similar materials that we had acquired at Caribbean and Panamanian sites, we flew to Genoa. There we were met by a physician, Guido Farris, whose avocation was the study and restoration of the pottery of his native area. Dr. Farris, urbane and aristocratic, called for us at our hotel in his racy sports car that he drove at breakneck speed down the *autostrada* while simultaneously carrying on a non-stop conversation in Italian that his English-educated son translated. The conference was being held at a lovely pink villa in nearby Savona, which had been long-weathered by the salty sea air into a streaked salmon color and was filled with antique furniture and the ghosts of another era. When Bob displayed the sherds we had brought with us, there was great excitement. These men, who for years had been talking to each other in glowing chauvinistic terms about "Genoa the Great," really had no inkling of the widespread distribution of their regional cultural evidence to the Western Hemisphere. They could relate our sherds to specifically known factories in the cluster of towns along the Ligurian coast, especially Savona, Albisola, and Genoa. When Bob told them that we were returning their wares after four hundred years, they seemed truly delighted. Suddenly, through archaeology and pottery, we had found a new common bond.

After the meeting, a large group took us to lunch at a local restaurant. Along with jugs of red wine and calamari, there were great heaping bowls of steaming pasta. A jocular man across the table who introduced himself as an artist tackled his spaghetti with such *gusto* that I was fascinated to watch him spin the stringy food around his fork with all the flourish of an orchestra conductor. Once he had somewhat snared it, he aimed his fork in the general direction of his mouth. Seeing pasta streaming down his chin and carbonara sauce dripping from ear to ear, I could not help but wonder about the table manners of all those other Italian artists whose works I had studied.

We passed that afternoon at the ruins of a castle that overlooks the old Genoa harbor. It was one of those places in Europe that were steeped in history. First came the Romans, then the Byzantines, then the men from the Middle Ages who wholeheartedly turned to the sea as their means of livelihood. They took fervent Crusaders to Asia Minor, shifted the commodities of the Mediterranean world from place to place, and finally controlled much of the trade in and out of Andalusia and the North African Maghreb. Our realm of interest concerned roomfuls of ceramics that had been recovered from the castle precincts, which were of exactly the same blue-on-blue type that we had known in the New

World. After studying these and the other styles we had found at the ceramic museum at Faenza and in the archaeological literature about recent diggings in Montelupo, a potting village near Florence, we were certain that Italian products had reached sixteenth- and seventeenth-century America.

Later in 1992, Genoa, claiming to be the boyhood home of Columbus, prepared a quincentennial celebration at which my kind Italian friends invited me to present a paper on their wares in the Americas. Although deeply touched, I could not bear to return alone.

For us, "Around the World in Eighty Days" was rearranged into "Around the World by Ship in a Full Semester, with 525 Undergraduate College Students," subtitled "How to Cope with the Usual Modern Campus Problems of Youthful Experimentation in Freedom, Sex, Booze, and Drugs, Coupled with Travelers' Diarrhea, Seasickness, and Cultural Shock." Why would two persons approaching that plateau euphemistically known as the Golden Years get involved in such an undertaking? Perhaps it was not only our incurable yen to travel and experience the trip by sea, but because we also did not realize how out-of-tune with young folks we had become during our long absence from the college scene. Moreover, there promised to be academic advantages to the research that for many years had consumed so much of our private time.

We signed on to teach aboard a floating college operated under the auspices of the University of Colorado. It utilized a large old vessel that was owned by a Chinese entrepreneur and manned by a Chinese crew. The purpose of the program was to expose the student body, which consisted of overwhelmingly upper-class Americans, to the Third World and to places in-between. In 1980 it was a sign of the times that the largest enrollments were for courses in business and in women's studies, which could just as easily have been studied on campus, and not in the subjects of history, anthropology, or geography, which could best be studied on location.

Bob offered two classes in the general anthropology or archaeology of the regions that we planned to visit. I gave a course in the history of world ceramics, confident that the universality of pottery would be particularly evident in those countries we were visiting that had not yet been seduced by more expensive plastics. The itinerary included three of the great ceramic areas of the world—Japan, China, and Greece.

In Japan we visited our first climbing kiln. Dozens of chambers snaked up a hillside beside a tiny group of houses that had traditionally been a pottery-making center for twelve generations. This kiln arrangement, which was designed to capitalize on the rise of heat, permitted artisans to attain much greater temperatures than was possible in the two-chambered, vertical kiln construction of the Mediterranean. It took Europeans centuries to understand that it was this extreme heat applied to kaolin clay and feldspathic glaze that caused the vitrification needed to create the translucent substance known as porcelain. We visited collections of some of the historical Japanese wares about which I was teaching but had never actually seen. This was what some might call staying one step ahead of the students.

In Taiwan our trip to a porcelain factory was disappointing because it turned out to be a totally modern, mechanized installation. Unquestionably, it was cleaner, more orderly, and more efficient than the Japanese factory had been, but it lacked the aura of the past's accumulated toil and experience. That disappointment was counterbalanced by an exhilarating day at the National Museum. When the Nationalist Chinese fled the mainland, they had taken with them most of the priceless treasures of one of the richest civilizations on earth, including what is perhaps the world's best representation of the 2000-year history of porcelain. This was not CEP, as experts refer to Chinese export porcelain, but instead, it was an overwhelming panorama of pieces so exquisite that they were meant for emperors. In a daze, I went from hall to hall hopelessly trying to absorb it all.

At another Taipei museum there was an outstanding exhibit of T'ang pottery, whose palette has particular significance for students of Islamic ceramics. That is because such pottery, which was decorated in splashes of green and yellow under a transparent lead glaze, reached ninth-century Mesopotamia through an active trade across the Indian Ocean. As one example of the complex global interactions of ceramic traits, potters at Baghdad and Samarra had sought to copy both the T'ang method and the white porcelaneous types that were being made contemporaneously in China. Reverberations of these stimuli then snowballed down through the centuries, eventually to reemerge in the central Mexican environment on the other side of the world.

A side trip from Hong Kong to Canton undertaken by a trainload of our group afforded us the chance of observing the continuous fundamental importance of pottery for daily Chinese life. Such use of ceramics ranged from the universal red roof tiles and bricks, to the rows of enormous water jars standing beside farm houses, to the garish temple decorations, to the tableware and soup spoons in our hotel dining room. In one market I purchased a simple, but large country jar after a toothless old crone plunged it into a tub of water to show that it did not leak.

A porcelain factory in an outlying town was operating by implementing a combination of both old and new methods. All products were made with molds and fired in saggars. In the decorating rooms, troops of women and girls sat tediously painting these mass-produced objects and then dipping them in vats of liquid glaze, all accomplished to the incongruous strains of piped-in German opera music. An enormous climbing kiln capable of holding thousands of pieces was incorporated into the center of the two-story structure, which created its own elevation. The town's residents must have been potters for centuries because every cut bank along the streets and every open patch of ground was a consolidated mass of broken pottery. If only I could have been turned loose there!

Next came the Philippines, where we encountered our first export porcelain. This was not unexpected. After Manila was founded, a large Chinese colony had set up businesses there as they customarily did all across southeast Asia. Among the other articles that were brought by junks from Canton, traveling down the Pearl River and then across the South China Sea, were porcelain jars, bowls, cups without handles, and many other domestic ceramics. A sizable assortment of these wares was available for viewing in the city museum. Many more could be found in the numerous antique stores. It would appear that hunting pots was a profitable occupation that the authorities were unable or unwilling to halt. While Bob drew a turn at desk duty on board our ship, I spent a day in the large library of the American Embassy perusing books not available at home that dealt with the Manila galleon trade to New Spain.

In Jakarta we found the most extensive CEP collection in that corner of the world. By then most of the types of the successive dynasties from Han to Ch'ing were familiar enough to me for sight recognition. I felt satisfied that I had completed my brief self-help program in this pottery as it related to our American and Spanish studies, but there was more pottery to come.

Near Bangalore, India, in a hamlet preparing for its 1000th birthday, a potter working in a dark hovel showed off his very crude wheel. It was made of stone, was set near ground level, and was propelled by his foot while he leaned over it in an awkward position to partially pull up a round-bodied jar. The wheel differed little from the throwing apparatus that had been recovered at Mohenjadaro in the Indus Valley and dated at ca. 4000 B.C. It spun at sufficient speed but oscillated badly, making the jar somewhat lopsided. This defect was obscured by finishing off the vessel with pats of a wooden paddle on the exterior while holding an anvil inside. Earlier we had seen such jars hanging against the trunks of certain kinds of palms to collect coconut juice for fermenting into a potent, raw-tasting beverage. Exactly the same ceramics that had been made in a comparable fashion were noted in Sri Lanka's open-air markets.

In Cairo we tried to revisit the potteries in Fustat, which had originally been destroyed during the eleventh century but were now occupied by squatters and where we had watched our first Muslim artisans seventeen years earlier. In order to reach them, however, it was necessary to wade across several acres of rotting, fly-clouded garbage. There are limits to my enthusiasm for ceramics, and that was one of them. The museum displays and the scenes from our bus as we traveled through the countryside served to remind me of the pottery that had been so much a part of our Nubian experience.

Greece provided us with a refresher course on the range of vessel forms that had been basic to subsequent ceramic developments everywhere in the Mediterranean basin. The torpedo-shaped amphorae modifications that some two millennia later carried millions of gallons of Andalusian wine across the Atlantic to thirsty colonists in the Americas had always fascinated me. Our final stop in Spain brought us full circle in our international search for information.

The university work that had made this pottery survey possible settled into a scheduled routine once we had cleared San Francisco Bay and gotten our sea legs. For the next three-and-a-half months, half of our time was spent at sea and half in thirteen different ports. To a certain degree, we were an isolated microcosm of American campus life in a series of extraordinary exotic settings that emphasized the frictions and the camaraderie that come with inescapable togetherness. The gregarious young adjusted better to the inevitable loud mob scene that attended most activities than did some of us older adults who had learned to place more value on privacy and silence. Except for Sunday, classes were held every day during sailing time. Like land-based professors, those of us aboard the S.S. *Universe* fretted about low academic standards and sluggish minds, yet we also realized that the cramped facilities, scores of distractions, and continuous excitement over what probably would be one of the great adventures of a lifetime made concentration difficult. In the evenings there were lectures or demonstrations by visiting regional artists, journalists, and government officials who traveled with us for various stretches of the route and spoke of some aspects of life in their homelands. One of these visitors was Arthur Clarke, author of *The Year 2001,* who boarded the ship at his hometown of Colombo and sailed with us to Cairo. Clarke caused quite a stir due to the brilliantly colored sarongs that he liked to wear, but it was his powerful shortwave radio that we most appreciated. Listening to it somewhere in the Indian Ocean, we first heard of Ronald Reagan's landslide presidential election. That evening the nightly student broadcast on the ship's closed circuit television featured the daughter of Joan and Ted Kennedy reading that news.

Shore time was special because it provided students and staff with a valuable break from the tensions of confinement and with eagerly awaited opportunities to see new people and places. There were optional short free trips and longer paid tours to points of general interest. Aside from the well-known monuments, these excursions included visits to Chinese farming communes and universities, to Indian silkworm farms and silk-weaving factories, to Balinese beaches, and to Ceylonese spice gardens. Most students also buckled on their backpacks and went off in small groups to explore on their own. They were encouraged to mingle with the local populace in order to gain some person-to-person insight into other cultures. Their success at this was enviable. By giving the children they met a few trinkets, such as balloons or pencils, and by exhibiting their unabashed friendliness, they were often invited into private homes for meals, weddings, and other celebrations. Later on board the ship, round-table discussions frequently showed a new perception of the social, political, and economic ills of some of the depressed sectors of the world, as well as a deepened respect for our American way. To more cynical adults, there was a touch of hypocrisy in their sincere commiseration, especially when one took stock of their expensive trekking gear and their customary battery of electronic gadgetry and then witnessed an astounding outpouring of capitalistic resources at each port that could have supported some of the poor families for whom their hearts bled for several weeks. The ship's hold was soon filled with their acquired purchases that included furniture, rugs, jade, silks, camel saddles, cameras, watches, jewelry, lacquer, ivory, and yes, even porcelain. But it was the planting of a germ of understanding and compassion that some time in the future might bear fruit. More entertaining for us were the unintended costume shows that occurred following each stop. After Japan, it was kimonos; after the Philippines, embroidered shirts and dresses; after Indonesia, batiks; after India, saris and silks; after Egypt, *jellabas* and turbans; after Greece, fisherman caps and coarsely knitted sweaters; and after Spain, berets.

With these hundreds of young people going off in all directions, eager to make the most of their free time and exotic surroundings, there was always the potential for trouble. They were quickly spotted as foreigners who were careless with their possessions, loose with their money, and reckless with their persons. During the history of the program there had been clashes with the law, drownings in dangerous waters, highway accidents, rapes, muggings, attempted drug smuggling, and other assorted horrors, which the students might or might not have avoided had they stayed at home. Our journey was no exception. In Egypt, a young lady lost her balance while climbing one of the pyramids and plummeted to her death. Off Florida, a boisterous fellow fell overboard and was rescued only because the alarm was sounded immediately, the seas were calm, and it was broad daylight.

The ship was usually scheduled to arrive in ports in the early morning hours. It was a good time to be out on deck to witness the skillful maneuvering of the landing tugs and the port activities and to have one's first view of a new horizon. Even so, it was still a special thrill one rosy December morning to glide into the calm Florida intercoastal waterway and tie up at the pier of Fort Lauderdale. As we waited a long day for the tons of baggage to be unloaded at customs, I wondered why I had not taken Bob's advice years ago and turned to collecting unbreakable, foldable textiles instead of my fragile ceramic treasures. I also smiled to myself about the treat in store for some unsuspecting parents whose daughters, while traveling in India, had acquired diamond nose studs.

Because the crux of our maiolica research centered around Spain, we made a number of trips to various parts of the country where maiolicas were known to have been made or where collections of medieval examples presently are housed. Even while realizing they were not being recovered at all or only in limited amounts in the Americas, we concentrated at first upon acquiring a broad background of all styles. This took us to Catalonia, the Levant, and Castile, but gradually our interests focused more intently upon the area of modern Andalusia. Its port city of Seville had enjoyed a tight monopoly on transatlantic commerce during much of the colonial era. A ceramic industry was recorded as having been active there. We expanded our inquiry to include more utilitarian earthenware from all periods of Andalusian history beginning with the Romans about the time of Christ. This long-range view was considered essential because of an amazing continuity of techniques, forms, and styles, that had lasted in some cases for many centuries regardless of what cultural entity happened to be in political control.

As we began our work in the late 1960s, however, Seville was a virtual ceramic no man's land. Few knew anything about the typical pottery that had formerly been made there except for the huge earthenware baptismal fonts, one of which was recovered in a small church in a suburb of Mexico City, and the many massive collars for household wells. Brightly colored tiles had long been regarded as a local specialty and were thought to have been dispersed into international markets. Other than those few ceramics, however, there was not much to go on. The emphasis everywhere was overwhelmingly either on the lusterware of the Muslim emirate of Granada that had been vanquished by Isabella and Ferdinand in the same year that Columbus first landed in the Caribbean or on the late sixteenth- through eighteenth-century maiolicas of Talavera de la Reina. At the time almost none of the former had been retrieved in the Americas, but the latter were considered a possibility that had to be explored.

The center of a Castilian agricultural district on the Tagus River about 100 miles southwest of Madrid, Talavera had blossomed into a thriving pottery-producing town during the reign of Philip II. At that time, the capital was being located in Madrid and the enormous austere Escorial was being constructed. Both undertakings demanded large amounts of decorated earthenware as furnishings for the quarters of the court and for wealthy citizens. This was especially the case after the bankrupt monarchy decreed that the ornate silver services acquired during the American conquests should be melted down in order to fill its empty coffers.

The Talavera industry prospered to such an extent that in time, it had completely swamped other regional potteries, except for those making coarse domestic utensils for on-the-spot consumption. The rise in importance of Talavera post-dated the introduction of ceramics to the New World by fifty years. Nevertheless, it is possible that the pottery made there before ca. 1550 or the later, low-grade wares that were meant for poorer customers might have been some of the same types that had been found during the Mexico City subway excavations or in early sixteenth-century Caribbean sites.

Alice Frothingham, an eminent American student of Spanish ceramics, identified similar tableware as Talaveran in a famous oil painting by Francisco de Zurbarán. When we showed an assortment of our Mexican sherds that were identical styles to Balbina Martínez Caviró, the director of a ceramic museum in Madrid, however, she scoffed at their crudeness and assured us that certainly no Talaveran potter would ever have been responsible for them and that quite surely they had to be inept colonial efforts!

In an attempt to sort out these conflicting opinions, we rented a car on several occasions to drive to Talavera. Getting through the traffic of Madrid was fearsome, but with Bob behind the wheel and me in the passenger seat serving as map and sign reader and only missing a few critical junctions, we successfully made our way into the countryside. As was our usual custom, we paused beside the road under a gnarled old tree for a bit of cheese, crackers, and wine, while feasting our eyes upon a grand vista sweeping across the dry plains of La Mancha. For Southwesterners, there is a sense of belonging in this part of Spain because the landscape is so similar to ours, except for a few castles and rolling hills dotted with olive trees.

At Talavera we found many factories making poor imitations of the old styles using molds and gas-fired kilns. No trace of the shops that had existed during the heyday of Talaveran ceramics was found and hence, no clue to the former technology. A ceramic museum lacked specimens comparable to those we carried, but one could detect some broadly shared stylistic nuances of them. Several churches retained wall panels of polychrome tiles dating from these periods, but beyond their basic concept, they did not seem particularly connected to what we knew had existed in Spanish America.

Our next stop on these excursions was always Oropesa, a tiny, walled community that is dominated by a lofty castle on a hill and looks every bit like a travel poster of romantic old Spain. Luckily for us, the castle, which had once been the home of a Peruvian governor, had been converted into an attractive government inn, or *parador,* with no more than half a dozen guest rooms and an excellent dining room. Using these dreamy surroundings as a base, we made our way to the hamlet of Puente del Arzobispo, where in times past rural potters had produced earthenwares like those in the larger Talavera. Old documents regulating prices revealed that Puente del Arzobispo ceramics had been less highly regarded and cheaper than the Talaveran pottery, suggesting that these might be the humble sort we had been seeking. Our visits to the workshops and our wanderings through the back streets of the town, however, turned up no concrete evidence of that. Finally as we stood watching artisans plying their craft, Bob casually asked one of them where their pottery wasters had been dumped. We reasoned that the modern disposal areas would likely be at or near the places that had traditionally been used in earlier times. The potter pointed toward the banks of the Tagus. At that spot it is a relatively shallow, slow-flowing stream that is slightly entrenched in the surrounding plain. The *puente* of the town's name refers to a Roman bridge that had been built across it.

Walking down into the cut of the river, we worked our way upstream around a bend, over drifts of modern rubbish, and around cows grazing by the water's edge before arriving at an embankment some forty feet high. Closer inspection through a growth of weeds and a thin blanket of fresh garbage revealed thick lenses of potsherds and clay cockspurs that had been used to separate glazed objects during firing and glued into the bank face by compacted soil, forming an astonishing deposit.

By its nature, archaeology thrives on trash—the more, the better. Recently discarded materials lose their repugnance through the desiccation and evaporation brought on by time, neither of which condition had yet prevailed in this instance. But in the interest of science, we excitedly began pulling pieces free from the mess covering them, using our pant legs to remove some of the surface dirt. A young lad riding a bike on the trail above us stopped to curiously watch the queer couple below groveling about through old shoes, bottles, plastic bags, smashed toys, dead birds, and orange rinds and picking up pieces of broken dishes. It seemed such fun that he joined us in our search.

We had apparently stumbled onto a layer of sixteenth- and seventeenth-century pottery. The recovered fragments matched those of the period that we had noted in the Talavera museum. As we reconstructed the situation, we de-

Banks of the Tagus River at Puente del Arzobispo in Castile are a loosely consolidated mass
of potsherds and kiln furniture representing at least three centuries of manufacture.

cided that from their beginning activities, Puente del Arzobispo pottery workers had carted their accumulated rejects and mishaps to the river's escarpment
at this location, tossed them over the side, and trusted in the forces of nature
to clean house every now and then. Like many housekeepers, however, the
Tagus had also overlooked some difficult waste pockets. Later in our travels
throughout the country, we saw that whenever Spanish pottery shops had existed near streams, their river banks had always served as convenient dumping
grounds. That is the way with research: Once a job is finished, answers that
would have been very helpful in the beginning suddenly appear.

Back at the *parador,* I washed sackfuls of the finds in the lavatory and then
tried to select only a representative collection, a difficult task, since it is often
hard to part with things that might have significance at some future time. The
early types, which were our primary concern at this time, were not among the
lot, but there were others with compositions and motifs reminiscent of some
Mexican renditions. As I packed away most of the sherds, I assured a skeptical
Bob that I really had tried to cull the selection.

On one of our drives to this region, we took the time to go farther into the rolling barren hills of Estremadura to Guadalupe, a place of interest to many Americans. It was to this shrine—a large church and cloister complex of golden stone squeezed into an isolated, constricted valley—that Columbus returned after his first voyage to give thanks for his success in arriving at Hispaniola's northern shore in just three months.

Our survey trips through Andalusia had given us a good idea of the tiles and other known ceramics of the area, but had revealed little information relevant to the specific kinds of pottery being recovered in the Americas. It was as if there had been two distinct categories of material goods, that of Andalusia and that of other provinces. Nevertheless, as our familiarity grew in proportion to the parameters of the research topic that we had outlined for ourselves, it was increasingly obvious that the ceramic history of that southern distriict was a most critical one. This was a pleasurable bonus because few would deny that from environmental and historical standpoints, this is the most fascinating part of Spain. A basic facet of this allure is that despite the homogeneous appearance of the *bourgeoisie* and of the phalanxes of high-rise apartments that afflict all of Western Europe, a cultural substratum in Andalusia has managed to retain its distinctiveness in dress, abode, and character in defiance of the twentieth century. We hoped that somewhere in those strata of the past, we would be perceptive enough to identify the old craft technology, if not the actual pottery.

Getting at the ceramic record, particularly in Seville, was not going to be easy. It was dispiriting that virtually no archaeology had been conducted within the city. This was due in part to a lack of interest by local scholars, who seemed to find the Andalusian handiwork of Roman sculptors and architects more entertaining than mucking around in later cultural deposits that had been beaten like an omelet through the millennia of building, tearing down, and rebuilding on the same spot. Then there was also a high water table beneath the city that had a habit of flooding out excavations and dissolving whatever stratigraphic levels might be discernible. One could not blame the diggers for choosing less overripened ground. We just wished we had been persuasive enough to convince some of them that it would be worthwhile to help define all of Andalusia's cultural roots, even those latter-day suckers that had volunteered and then flowered in the New World.

After realizing that we were not apt to make converts to our cause, our success on the banks of the Tagus nevertheless caused us to look forward to compensating for the dearth of archaeological materials by making our own sherd finds along the Guadalquivir River that embraced Seville. The principal group of workshops is documented as having been just behind the western bank, opposite of the city. We now also knew that the pottery wasters would have been dumped there. As we arrived in Seville to come to grips with the problem, however, we found that we had already been outdone—first, by nature on the rampage; and second, by modern engineering efforts to cope with it. Time and again during Seville's long history, flood waters had taken the river from its meandering channel and rushed it through town, flushing away ceramics and other debris in the process. At last during the 1930s, the river's channel had been straightened so that it no longer posed a threat to the citizens. Gradually most of the river's exposed banks that had divided the city from its ancient potter's district were covered with concrete embankments and esplanades. The one riverside deposit of ceramics that we did see was created by a post-Napoleonic factory that made English-style transfer wares.

Our next hope was for a find in Seville's great cathedral, a huge confection of stony spires and flying buttresses that had loomed over the city for four-and-a-half centuries. The square bell tower that stood beside it was the minaret of a Berber mosque. Exemplary of the conservative attitudes of Andalusia, it had been built in the Gothic style two centuries after that mode was abandoned in France, where it had originated. Archival notations from the late fifteenth and early sixteenth centuries confirmed that the masons working on this structure had followed a practice introduced to Spain by the Romans, which involved using earthenware as ballast above the vaulting. When certain sections of the structure reached the roofing stage, potters had sold wagonloads of all types of complete and broken vessels from their shops and waster dumps to the church authorities for this purpose. The fifty or so years during which this transfer was taking place coincided exactly with the era of the *conquistadores* and also, therefore, with the Spanish ceramics that had been introduced in the Americas. There was no doubt in our minds that the enormous volume of pottery that had been stored away in the superstructure of this landmark—the world's largest Gothic cathedral—represented a definitive solution to some of our academic problems.

Enormous Gothic cathedral dominating Sevillian skyline likely has fifteenth- and sixteenth-century pottery incorporated in its fabric. The separate belltower is at its base a twelfth-century Muslim minaret topped by a sixteenth-century Catholic superstructure.

Knowing that it was possible to enter the roof structure of some French Gothic cathedrals by means of catwalks over the vaulting, we armed ourselves with letters of introduction to the Archbishop of Seville that explained our research and asked the Church's permission for us to conduct limited explorations. After having worked on top of a Mexican cathedral, we thought it would just be an extension of our research to work inside a Spanish one. Unfortunately, however, what had sounded so reasonable to us in New Mexico, proved to be impossible on the scene in Seville.

Climbing up the Giralda bell tower and looking down upon the massive Seville cathedral below, we saw at once that there was no roof over the vaulting. In the temperate climate of Andalusia, which did not include the destructive problems of freezing and thawing, the exterior curvature of the vaults had simply been bricked and left exposed. The ceramic ballast had been effectively sealed from below and from above and would only be available in the event of a disaster to the building. Dejectedly, I stood in the cathedral's cavernous dark interior, craning my neck to peer up at its lofty shadowed ceiling, and inwardly cursed the frustrating irony of having our goal so near at hand and yet so totally out of reach.

We persistently canvassed the local museums, and things began to look up as we were passed from one staff member to another. Our sack of sherds, which had been obtained beneath Mexico City and were judged to be colonial in Madrid, were unhesitatingly claimed as local products in Seville. Locating substantiation for this opinion was troublesome, however, because such pottery held no interest for students or for the public. Gradually a few pieces were found tucked away and forgotten on dusty basement storage shelves. They were coarse white or blue-on-white maiolica plates and small bowls that had been retrieved during the course of various municipal projects, such as street repair or the laying of sewer lines. They could not be dated. Nevertheless, it was important for our studies that they were present in Seville and in its environs, but had been found nowhere else as far as we were able to ascertain.

A real turning point in our quest came at the Museum of Fine Arts, where we examined an early seventeenth-century Zurbarán oil painting, *The Miracle of Saint Hugh* (1629), that depicted dishes attributed to Talavera. Shown on a table before some Carthusian priests wearing pristine white robes were small bowls of a style identical to some we had just found in Seville's storage rooms and to others we knew from the Americas. Zurbarán also portrayed some two-handled jars bearing the crest of the Seville chapter of the Order. The painting had been commissioned by a Carthusian monastery, which was located across the river from the city and until recently had housed the transfer ware factory that had taken over the earlier abandoned buildings. The Carthusians owned a number of medieval houses in town where potters had set up their workshops. One might assume that the dishes the priests used had come from those tenants. The fact that Zurbarán worked a century after the opening phase of the colonial period only served to illustrate the extraordinary persistence of some Spanish ceramic styles, particularly among low-caliber wares.

In commenting upon all of this to the museum's staff, we learned that shortly before our visit, a Carthusian friar from Jérez de la Frontera, sixty miles south of Seville, had brought some actual pieces of similar pottery to them, saying they had been found in the Jérez cloister. Because they were like those in the painting of his earlier Brothers, the priest thought that the museum might like

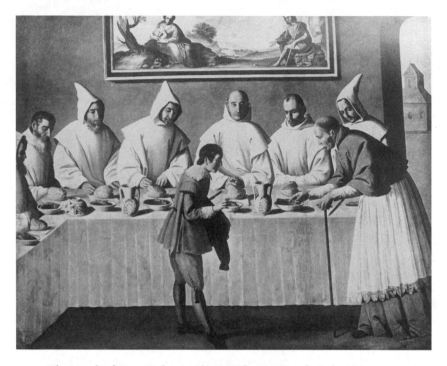

The Miracle of Saint Hugh painted in 1629 by Francisco de Zurbarán portrays maiolica pottery vessels identical to late fifteenth- and early sixteenth-century types recovered archaeologically from sites in New Spain.

to display them to demonstrate the artist's accuracy. But of course, our museum host shrugged, this was far too crude a pottery to exhibit in an art gallery, wasn't it? The painting was greatly prized as a masterpiece of the Siglo del Oro, but the pottery portrayed in it was another matter. He could give us a letter of introduction to the priest, however, if we wished to see for ourselves just what had been unearthed in the Jérez cloister. Would we ever!

On our second try, we were greeted at the massive wooden door of the Jérez Carthusian monastery by two priests. They were a Don Quixote and Sancho Panza pair. The priest in charge was an elderly man with a tall, thin build and a satisfying ascetic appearance. His rotund, squat companion looked to me as if he would have been more at ease behind a team of oxen than on his knees before an altar. Both wore white serge robes that had gone a long time between cleanings, and it flashed through my mind that with his keen eye for accuracy, Zurbarán may have graciously overlooked such mundane details.

Their Order had the reputation for strict austerity, not allowing its members any contact with the outside world through radio, television, newspapers, or even personal letters. We therefore did not know just what our reception might be. To our relief, however, the priests were very cordial, perhaps because they had few opportunities to converse with outsiders, especially with foreigners. They were happy to allow Bob to examine and photograph their pottery, but the lady, they indicated, pointing at me, would have to remain outside. Bob therefore followed them alone behind the towering walls, loaded down with his camera, drop cloth, reference scale, recorder, and notebook.

Frustrated once again, I ambled up to the Baroque portal and entered the walled atrium in front of the elegant façade of the chapel, which is now a national monument. A riot of purple bougainvillea hung over a wall that was adorned with a tiled plaque of scenes illustrating La Cartuja's history. One view was of the miraculous discovery of a statue of the Virgin within a domed kiln. I took that as a good omen for our inquiry.

Across the road from the church complex I saw some tilled fields. Early in my adventures as a pottery student, I learned that near archaeological zones, the plow is often a good friend to the archaeologist. So it was in that Jérez vineyard. The ground was speckled with fragments of the types of maiolica that interested us—the first I had seen since we arrived in Spain. It was important that in addition to obtaining a study collection for ourselves, we also needed to secure a sample for the comparative physical analyses of clays that would be conducted by chemists at the Smithsonian Institution. Therefore, I fell to the task with a vengeance, gathering bits of the pottery into the plastic bags that I had learned to carry in my purse as others carry Kleenex. After a while, I became aware of a scattering of thin red sherds that I had overlooked in my concentration on the maiolicas. Although there was no sign of any Roman remains in the vicinity, I knew that this part of Spain had been Roman territory for six hundred years, and I recognized at once that these sherds were *terra sigillata*. For a displaced Southwesterner such as I, finding Roman pottery was a special thrill, since it dated from a time before any Anasazi had ever dreamed of combining clay with heat to produce containers.

Two hours later Bob emerged from the monastery looking as if he had been put through the wringer. While his hosts, their breaths heavy with garlic, had simultaneously bombarded him with conversation and explanations in rapid

Carthusian priests walking in cloisters at Jérez de la Frontera who salvaged from their establishment fifteenth-century pottery that was produced in Sevillian workshops

Spanish, he had experienced his first solo attempt at picture- and note-taking, trying at the same time to be attentive, think in Spanish, and remember all the picayune details about which he knew I was sure to ask. He learned that for many years the priests had been restoring their cloisters following a century of abandonment. This work involved trenching around foundations and cleaning out wells. A great deal of pottery, much of it unbroken or restorable, had been preserved. The two priests had interested themselves in this earthenware and made one cell of their compound into a pottery display area for the sole benefit of their fellow Carthusians.

Among other things, the priests had amassed a collection of approximately three dozen bowls, plates, and two-handled jars that were identical to those in

Carthusian monastery at Jérez de la Frontera, Spain, whose cloisters constructed
in the fifteenth century yielded ceramics of same kind and quality as
those taken to the Americas by Spanish conquistadors

the Zurbarán painting, except that the jar crest was that of the Jérez rather than
of the Seville Order. Of crucial importance to us were the facts that the construction of the monastery had occurred during the latter decades of the fifteenth century and that, because Jérez had then just been a village, the furnishings had likely been brought from the regional commercial center of Seville.
Without much doubt, the recovered maiolicas represented the output of that
urban industry. We were jubilant to learn that most of the basic types in which
we were interested were present. Therefore, between the sherds I had picked
up and the photos we had taken of complete vessels in Seville and now also in
Jérez, we felt that this phase of our mission had come to a reasonably successful conclusion. We were also confident that we had pinned down Seville as the
prime supplier for the earthenware that was sent to the Americas.

We went off to unwind and savor our good fortune at the nearby charming,
walled hilltop settlement of Arcos de la Frontera. Bob headed the car up the
narrow one-way street into town, helped by mirrors mounted on building walls

to enable drivers to see around blind corners. As we emerged onto a small treeless plaza, the bells of the large church facing it began to ring. The Christians were still proclaiming their sovereignty over what—as the town's name implied—had been a bloody thirteenth-century frontier separating them from the retreating infidels. Andalusians are not a people to forget their history.

Eight years were to pass before we could return to La Cartuja at Jérez to reconfirm our original opinions and be updated on the finds that had been made subsequent to our first visit. The old priest was too frail to meet us, but Sancho Panza was there, still happy and still smelling of garlic. As he and an associate again escorted Bob inside the cloisters, Bob called over his shoulder for me to stand at the entrance. He would try to bring specimens to the door so that I could also see them, a sort of analysis by remote control. Soon a double-doored gate farther down the building opened, and a lay workman on a tractor appeared. Upon seeing me standing there, he frantically motioned me away, apparently fearing that my curious eyes would steal a glimpse into that mysterious masculine world behind the walls.

In a few minutes, Bob and the priests called to me. They had with them more clues to add to the network of evidence that we were slowly accruing. One was a fragile bowl of the Ligurian blue-on-blue vogue. This was the first complete example of the Italian style that we had seen in Spain. Bob showed the clerics a picture of a nearly identical object that had been found in the mud of the cathedral compound beneath Mexico City. They all marveled at the distant straying of such delicate things. Another vessel was a Chinese porcelain teacup without handles, one of about a dozen that had been found dumped down a patio well. These cups were later identified as being from the seventeenth century. Zurbarán, faithful to the truth, had included such a cup turned upside down on the table in his painting. His specimen had shown a faint hairline crack up one side, as if to symbolize the priestly denunciation of worldly riches. Little porcelain had previously been found in Andalusia, making these Carthusian articles notably significant.

On this trip we had brought a copy of a monograph that contained some of the photographs Bob had taken during our first encounter with the Carthusians. Back inside the cloisters, the priests obviously were pleased as they went from pictures to pots and recognized old friends. After both visits they had thoughtfully presented us with some small gifts from the sequestered collection. These remained special trophies to us because of the appreciation those hermetically isolated priests demonstrated for the universal language of pottery. A loving prize also came as we departed for the final time. Sancho Panza handed Bob a minute sixteenth-century blue-on-white bowl, probably intended as a salt cellar. With a puckish grin, he said, "This is for the *señora* to use for drinking her whiskey!" Laughing at his little outside joke, he and his companion waved as they retreated once more back behind their sheltering walls. We drove away, content with our precious data and with the friendship, through pottery, of two kind gentlemen.

In the Seville environs we had already found confirmation for the manufacture of specific pottery types distributed in the Spanish New World, but it was in Granada that we were most successful in reconstructing the technology that had produced them. Of the three trips that we made there, the one during autumn after the throngs of tourists had thinned out was the most pleasant. We obtained lodgings in the charming *parador,* which was located in a sixteenth-century convent that had been built adjacent to the Nasrid's Alhambra palace by the Catholic Kings to affirm the totality of their reconquest. From there, we strolled at our leisure through various parts of the monument, naturally paying attention to the dazzling dado panels of *alicatado* mosaic tile running from the salons to the courtyards of the edifice. We had already seen such *alicatado* tile in some Moroccan buildings that also dated from the thirteenth century.

At the Spanish Muslim museum, which was housed in some rooms of the Renaissance structure Charles V erected almost within the Alhambra, we examined Nasridian ceramics. The most notable that we saw was the famous lusterware that was considered to be a Persian contribution to Spanish ceramic art. We also prowled the extensive landscaped grounds of the Alhambra precincts, eyeing the cultivated flower beds for potsherds, but our search was only moderately successful.

More interesting for our purposes was a complex of small kiln sites to which the museum director, Jesus Bermúdez Pareja, led us. Only the combustion chambers remained. This was to be expected because such structures customarily were at least partially subterranean with the surrounding earth serving as a buttress against the firing heat's destructive forces. The upper chambers where the pots were baked were located above ground. Since they were not reinforced, they must have required periodic rebuilding. Once abandoned, they had fallen into rapid disrepair due to natural deterioration or acts of vandalism. In the case of the kilns on the Alhambra grounds, once the combustion units were exposed, it had been necessary to protect them, since even fire-hardened earth will collapse given sufficient moisture. For such stabilization, the pits had been lined with bricks. This gave them a regularity of form, with the walls squared up and made vertical, which likely was not their original condition. Some had a lateral tunnel approach for insertion of fuel. The effect from above was that of a keyhole shape to the lower half of the kilns. Although the cluster of these five or six kilns lies nearly directly beside the path leading from the Alhambra to the *Generalife* palace, there is no sign informing the public about what these remains represent. As a result, no visitors give them a glance, which is just as well for seekers of sherds such as we.

Cleared out during the 1930s, the kilns produced a few sherds that had sketchily been reported upon at the time. During successive administrations, however, they had been lost. Primarily, they were considered to be representative of Nasridian domestic ceramics; however, there was also some evidence for squatter reuse of the kilns during the troubled years that followed the departure of the defeated royal entourage in 1492. It seems that a white-ground maiolica style had been made before and after this fateful event, and we luckily found some examples that had weathered out in the years after exploration. This maiolica with its brick-red dense paste differed decidedly from the Spanish materials that had been recovered in the Americas, since both Sevillian and American finds had a light whitish to pinkish caste and a lightweight, porous nature. Granadan shops were ruled out as suppliers of New World maiolicas, but they had clearly made ceramics by similar methods.

The retracing of those methods next took us on a long walk down the very steep path from the hilltop location of the Alhambra, to the narrow Duero River valley at the base of the escarpment, and then up an opposite hill into what was left of the former Muslim quarter, or *albaicín*. The streets were cobbled and wound around the steep slope. Because the adjacent buildings were no more than several stories high, we did not get the feeling of being down in the bottom of some unfathomable canyon as we had in Seville's oldest sectors. We slowly made our way up through the knot of white houses and small business establishments to the remnants of the ancient city walls. A short distance away were two operating potteries, where we were told that traditional methods were still being used. In Granada, it seemed likely that traditional also meant Muslim.

We toured the largest of these shops on two occasions, once when work was actively under way and once when a sole caretaker let us wander freely through the idle premises. Although this shop was geared almost exclusively to making maiolicas, we gained from it a feeling for the systems and rhythms of work that we had not fully appreciated in the other Andalusian pottery workshops we had visited.

Within the Granada workshop compound, the raw clay came in, was processed, was allowed to ripen, and then was thrown, trimmed, dried, baked, decorated, rebaked, packed, and sold. With the exception of motorized grinding mills, there was little to distinguish the tools or procedures from centuries past. It was a mass production, assembly-line enterprise based upon the economics of supply and demand, whose employees were assigned certain prescribed tasks for which they needed long, specialized training and for which they were paid wages. Not merely in the use of the potter's wheel and the kiln, but also in almost every other way, it was a far different craft activity from that of a few housewives making kitchen utensils for their own use. The aspect of the Granada pottery-making technology that most interested us was the placement of the potters' kick wheels. Imagine my delight upon seeing that they were located in trenches in the throwing room's dirt floor, just as they had been in Morocco. Inasmuch as library research indicated that such pit wheels had existed elsewhere in Muslim Spain, there remained no doubt in my mind that such wheels had also been used in Seville at the end of the fifteenth century and in the first pottery workshops set up in Mexico.

During the days of the Franco dictatorship, Spain had been a safe place for travelers because street crime was not tolerated. After the old general was gone, however, lawless elements quickly saw to it that Spain sank to the disturbing level of the Western democracies. This was brought home to us when the S.S. *Universe* docked for three or four days in Málaga. A dozen students reported their backpacks being slashed and items stealthily stolen as they walked along the streets. A faculty family driving a rental car stopped for a traffic signal, whereupon two youths smashed the car's rear hatchback window and made off with their purse and briefcase. When we later returned to Spain, numerous persons ranging from our hotel maids to our archaeological colleagues, warned us to be especially cautious. Tourists were the prime targets of pickpockets and hotel thieves. Consequently, I never carried a handbag, and whenever we needed a camera, Bob clutched it to his chest with the shoulder strap well-concealed beneath his jacket collar. We also took taxis to and from our destinations rather than walking, which had always been our usual custom.

By following these precautions, we encountered only one alarm. Unable to flag a cab at the Granada factory, we strolled back to town through the *albaicín*, camera secured to Bob's chest. We emerged into modern Granada at the small plaza at the foot of the Alhambra hill. As we ambled along toward the provincial archaeological museum, we paused to look into a store window that was filled with pottery from the workshop we had just visited. I happened to glance back over my shoulder straight into the eyes of a man standing a few feet behind us who seemed to be intently watching us. He immediately looked away, pretending to peer at a store's merchandise. We moved on. So did he. When we stopped at another storefront, he was right behind us, standing at the window we had just left. To break this cat-and-mouse pattern, I stepped inside a shop on the pretext of examining some items on sale. Bob stood in the doorway looking at the people in the plaza and watching out of the corner of his eye for signs of impending disaster. Our follower paused several steps away, biding his time. After waiting a few minutes, he apparently had second thoughts and drifted off across the square to lose himself in the crowd. Still somewhat fearful, we hurried down a deserted street toward the museum. Three teenagers soon passed us, laughing and talking as they pranced down the center of the pavement, obviously harmless and oblivious to us. We stepped in right behind them and used them as an escort all the rest of the way. One mugging on behalf of science had been quite enough.

Lying off the Atlantic coast of Morocco, the Canary Islands had surely been key steppingstones in the spread of Andalusian pottery to the Americas. Spanish settlers arriving during the last quarter of the fifteenth century had quickly killed off most of the aboriginal population and with it, any source of earthenware supply necessary for carrying on daily life. Besides that, they showed no inclination for making their own utensils and instead, had such furnishings dispatched to them from the potteries beside the Guadalquivir. Once transatlantic trade commenced, the islands had become a required stop for the outbound galleons, all of which were outfitted at Seville. We therefore reasoned that there would be discarded ceramics linking the Indies with the motherland from both the colonists and from the commercial traffic. This was a premise that had to be proven by on-site observation, since no publications of any sort had dealt with this question.

After one field session in Andalusia, we took a bus from Seville to Cádiz. There we were to board a ship bound for the Canaries. As we pulled into the bus terminal at the port, we could see a large white vessel anchored a short distance away. Reaching this boat required considerable exertion on our parts, since both our luggage and our bodies had grown fat over the preceding six or seven weeks. As we puffed up to the pier, we suddenly heard the unmistakable sounds of barked orders and marching feet. A large contingent of soldiers was approaching from the opposite direction. They also carried gear, but were far less out of breath than some of us bystanders. As the police held back the boarding passengers, they filed right up the gangplank! Well now, that was a surprise. We had thought we were bound for a vacation paradise.

For the last few days the television in our Seville hotel lounge had carried pictures of gun-waving Moroccans crowded into trucks and other commandeered vehicles that were pouring over their country's southern desolate border into the Spanish Sahara. It seemed that the Spanish soldiers in our midst, all of whom were elite paratroopers, were going to the front on, of all things, a car ferry! Whatever happened to the glorious Spanish Navy that had once ruled the seas? Was there no sense of crisis demanding official transport? Perhaps the incident was not as serious an invasion as the newsmen had made out. As we saw the situation, once they arrived in the islands, these warriors would be flown by military aircraft on the short hop eastward to Spain's colonial enclave on the northwestern African coast. There they would descend upon the surprised enemy, who hardly would have expected reinforcements to arrive by public conveyance. In any case, if the paratroopers took over the battlefield as completely as they did our ship, it would be a very brief encounter.

At the same time, another event of national importance was occurring. After ruling Spain for thirty-eight years, General Franco lay dying. For several weeks medical news concerning his condition had dominated the papers and the radio broadcasts. We were personally apprehensive because we did not know what to expect in the event of his death. Would there be civil unrest? Surely at the very least, there would be a prolonged period of official mourning that would close down the government institutions with which we were dealing. Unanticipated delays could play havoc with our tight schedule. Fortunately, however, we had time to accomplish the work we had set out to do. On board ship, the frequent medical bulletins continued, but we observed that they were not interesting enough for the Spaniards to interrupt their favorite pastime of talking to each other.

Sailing out of Cádiz harbor into a fiery red sunset, we were following a course that Spanish sailors had taken for three centuries. The voyage took most sailing vessels a week to complete, but our modern craft cut that time in half. Early in the misty dawn of the third day, we went up on deck to watch our ship's prow glide into Santa Cruz on the craggy island of Tenerife. The town was strung along a shallow shelf of land, above which a forbidding mountain mass rose abruptly away from the sea.

Not surprisingly, our preconceptions of the Canary Islands had been based upon travel brochures that featured waving palms, brilliant bougainvillea cascading down the walls, and blooming poinsettias growing higher than a house. And indeed, that flora is present in some protected places along the shores and lower slopes, but it was all introduced, along with the cash crops of grapes and sugar cane. Prior to the arrival of Andalusians and Italians, most of the islands had been bleak, jagged reminders of ancient volcanic activity, having only thin soil, sparse vegetation, and no running streams. They had also been the native habitat of a particular species of wild canine, and the name of the island chain was derived from that source, not from the presence of warbling birds.

Presumably known since Classical times, these seven specks of land have often been referred to as the Fortunate Islands, since their climate is more evenly temperate than most of the Mediterranean basin. In archaeological terms, however, they have not been so fortunate. The reduced soil mantle did not permit any depth of cultural deposit, and repeated tidal waves and volcanic activity often eradicated what little deposit there was. Moreover, local scientists were not interested in the European period. When we showed our shopworn sherds to the curator of the Tenerife Museum, he vaguely recognized the type, but had no comparative specimens or personal knowledge, despite the fact that the first Spanish occupation had been at La Laguna, only a short distance up the slopes. He suggested Garachico on the opposite side of the island as a more promising place for our inquiry.

A three-hour bus ride brought us to Garachico. It had been an important port for the American trade up until the early eighteenth century. At that time a great wave of lava had rolled down the mountain that was behind the town, going into the ocean and also completely obliterating the settlement. Subsequently, with characteristic human tenacity, the inhabitants had erected new homes on either side of the flow, and life was resumed.

We called on the Garachico mayor, who in turn put us in touch with a gentleman said to be the local historian. We found him to be a grizzled, talkative old fellow, who rattled off an exceedingly rapid dialectic Spanish. The fact that he was toothless made him even more difficult to understand. By showing him our trusty sherds and photographs, we were able to gather that he knew our pottery well. He told us that when he was a boy, he and some of his friends had found a large bubble in the eighteenth-century lava field that exposed one room of an engulfed house. In the room they had discovered some whole earthenware pots. The youngsters had taken them outside, set them up on the rocks, and used them as targets until they were smashed. Boys will be boys around the world, but nevertheless, such stories make archaeologists cringe. Come to think of it, the old man decided, there might be some pieces of the same kind of pottery in his *bodega*. Hurrah!

Our informant then led us down a broad, monumental stone staircase beside the house to what once had been a private chapel. Inside it was an architectural gem, with a beautiful *mudéjar* wooden ceiling and enough carved and gilded altar pieces to send an antique dealer into ecstasy. Presently, however, the building was being used as a jumbled warehouse. Stacked about in utter confusion were crates, baskets, broken furniture, empty bottles, worn automobile tires, and assorted junk. Our guide poked about aimlessly, pulling out drawers, moving items around, and raising clouds of dust. Quickly tiring of the search, he announced that the pottery had been lost. There was a strong possibility that it was there somewhere, but under the circumstances, we could not press the issue. Before we stepped outside, he brushed a foot through the dirt beneath him to expose a floor of multicolored Sevillian tile, a gesture that seemed to tease us unmercifully.

Thanking our host for his courtesy, we dejectedly walked down to the shore to pass time before the bus came back on its return trip. Once again we had that helpless feeling of being so close to a goal and yet so far away. Then suddenly, on a narrow beach below the sea wall, the situation improved. Washed up against the wall were fragments of familiar sixteenth-century white and blue-on-white Sevillian maiolicas, as well as several blue-on-blue Italian pieces. It was not much of a haul—just a handful—but we could at least relax in the positive knowledge that our idea of diffusion to the Indies via the Canaries had been correct.

Those few finds gained even more importance after we flew to the island of Gran Canaria, the other major center of colonial Spanish occupation, since our various searches there turned out to be fruitless. Our disappointment was intensified because of personal problems. Although we had made a long-standing, confirmed reservation at a beach hotel, on arrival, no room was available. Once we showed them our written confirmation, however, a room was miraculously found for us in the mysterious way of hotel clerks. It was for one night only instead of the four for which we had arranged. Thereafter, every time we walked out of the hotel past the desk, an employee would stop us to say that we would have to go elsewhere. Then when we came back to the hotel, we had been moved into another room. We never knew where we would be, but each time we were moved, the accommodations became less desirable as we progressed from the front to the rear of the building. The reason behind such annoying treatment may have been that the beach was overcrowded with European vacationers. That must have been a permanent condition, however, judging from the signs for restaurants, cabarets, and shops along the esplanade that were written in German, Swedish, French, or English. One would scarcely have known that this was a part of Spain. It was a carnival not to our liking, and it made us even more anxious to leave.

Because our flight back to Madrid was scheduled for very early morning, we made arrangements to be picked up by taxi at about five a.m. We came down to the lobby to find ourselves in a ridiculous situation. A taxi was waiting, and a sleepy night clerk had aroused himself to hand Bob an erroneous bill. We had been charged for deluxe accommodations for the entire stay and for extraneous charges we had not incurred. Bob refused to pay. The clerk shrugged, saying there was no one he could call at that hour to explain the billing.

As an argument began to heat up, the taxi driver carried one bag out to the car, and I followed with our assorted hand luggage. The driver slumped down in the front seat and lit a cigarette. He seemed so unconcerned about our dilemma that I suspected he and the night clerk were partners in this scheme against hapless tourists. It was probably repeated every day. Bob did not appear; so I walked back to the hotel entrance. The door was locked! The clerk had flipped the inside bolt to prevent Bob from escaping with his suitcase. Through the glass, their angry faces and gestures told me that matters had not been resolved. As the minutes of our leeway time relentlessly ticked away, the clerk, door key in hand, knew that he had the advantage. Ultimately Bob was forced to relent and dig out the required *pesetas,* vowing loudly that, by damn, he was going to lodge an immediate complaint with the director of the National Tourist Office. Of course, he never did, but he did add that fracas to his growing list of pottery-related predicaments.

By the fall of 1983 it was time to wrap up the Spanish pottery project. Not that we had gotten all of the answers, but we had amassed so many details that we were fearful of running out of steam before they could be assimilated and prepared for publication. Our decision to publish necessitated a final trip to Spain to double-check our data and to obtain new photographs. We had also learned of subway construction beneath old Seville, which we hoped would produce as many ceramic sherds as such work in Mexico City had done.

A preliminary period was spent fighting the bureaucratic battles of Madrid. In seeking permission to photograph museum specimens, we were shunted from office to office and given such evasive answers that we finally gave up in despair and threw ourselves upon the mercy of Juan Zozaya, curator of Islamic ceramics at the National Archaeological Museum, who emphatically declared that administrators were the soulless enemies of researchers. Then he made it possible for us to obtain any pictures we needed of vessels that were on display or in storage. It was another bond of friendship made possible by a mutual interest in archaeological ceramics and their revelations.

Buoyed by that good fortune, we were off to Seville. There we found a new young museum director, Fernando Fernández, who was equally as cooperative.

We were given complete access to all materials available in the provincial archaeological museum. Don Fernando, as his employees called him, gave us the bad news that the subway project had been aborted before any appreciable artifact collection could be gathered. Some buildings near the two excavation sites where work had commenced soon showed such severe cracking from the construction vibrations that many had become afraid for the great cathedral, before which the subway line was to pass. Subsurface water at the depth necessary for tunneling also proved to be a major engineering obstacle.

To compensate for this disappointment, Don Fernando lifted our spirits with the announcement that there had been three archaeological excavations within the old city during the interval since our last visit. These activities had been undertaken because a new federal regulation required archaeological examination of the grounds of any building torn down in historical districts. Because Andalusia had suffered a prolonged drought, Seville's troublesome water table lowered enough to make stratigraphic controls in such spots more feasible, since these explorations were generally shallower than those proposed for the subway. At last, a small group of professionals and students was seriously concerning itself with local ceramics.

Work was still being conducted at one locality to which Don Fernando and his wife guided us. What had been uncovered illustrated the richness and the complexity of cultural deposits in a city that had been intensively occupied for as long as Seville. A nineteenth-century house had been demolished on a lot about twenty-five by one hundred feet in size. At the time of our visit, diggers had gone down some nineteen feet in the front of the cleared lot, where they encountered possible third- to fifth-century Roman remains. In the center of the cleared space, Muslim deposits that dated from about the eighth to mid-thirteenth centuries were being exposed. At the rear, the destroyed house foundations had punched through materials left from the longer Christian Era. It was pottery, however, that essentially distinguished these various occupations, and it was pottery that most obviously reflected the changes in social habits from one horizon to another. I was bemused to see a table of young ladies carrying on the customary feminine role of tediously labeling potsherds from these various levels. That was just where I had begun nearly half a century earlier.

The vacant lot on which this archaeological work was being conducted was surrounded on three sides by two- and three-story buildings, and it faced onto

*Studying fifteenth-century winged amphorae at the
provincial archaeological museum in Seville*

a street that was just wide enough to accommodate one car and was bordered
by a sidewalk of one-person width. If any vehicle came along, a pedestrian was
well-advised to turn sideways. All the dirt from the diggings was taken by wheelbarrows five blocks through a maze of alleyways to a small plaza that was spacious enough for a truck to enter. Presumably whenever a new home was erected
on the lot, some dirt would have to be returned in the same laborious manner.

Since Don Fernando had to make an inspection trip the next day to a site
south of town where the provincial authorities had a small crew at work, he
invited us to accompany him. Three Roman kilns were part of a large occupational zone there. Kilns of that period had been relatively common along the
banks of the Guadalquivir and its tributaries. Primarily they had produced

Excavations in nineteenth-century house foundations in old Seville,
with student assistants in background

earthenware amphorae in which the wine and olive oil of Andalusia had been
bottled, sent by ship down river, and then exported east through the Mediterranean to Rome. The amphorae themselves have significance for students of
later Spanish ceramics because their derivatives have continued to be used
through the ages, eventually reaching American shores by the millions. We
had not had any previous opportunity for seeing a kiln construction where
such objects were introduced to Spain, so we eagerly agreed to go along. Later
we almost wished we had not done so, since what we saw there was a kind of
make-work effort that was both detrimental to science and a wanton vandalism of antiquities.

Each of the so-called excavators at the site of Orippo had a shovel and was
spading up a patch of hard earth. There was no other excavation or surveying
equipment on hand and no indication that this was anything other than ran-

Removing spoil dirt from a densely occupied part of old Seville
(behind temporary brick wall) involved use of a wheelbarrow brigade

dom digging. No one was taking measurements, making notes or maps, or recording specimens. Hence, there could also be no meaningful interpretation of the previous periods of occupation. The sector in which the men were shoveling was an outlying part of a Roman village that had been situated on a low hill on the Guadalquivir's eastern bank. That hill is now an olive grove that exhibits no exposed Roman architectural features, but does contain the remains of a twelfth-century Muslim watchtower. As we approached, the men had just uncovered another item, which was common in Andalusia, but which we had never before seen. It was a human burial within an amphora. The vessel had been sliced vertically to permit the insertion of a corpse, in this case an infant. Then the jar was buried without a marker. We were told that dozens of similar interments had been found nearby, but that none had been accompanied by offerings of any kind. We therefore concluded that this had probably been a pauper's cemetery.

As for the kilns, which were located on the opposite slope of the hill next to a meander in the river that was cut off from the main channel farther west, two had been so nearly destroyed in recent times that they were covered with soil to forestall further damage. The third consisted only of a large, circular subterranean combustion chamber. It had been perforated on its upper surface to allow heat to flow into the now absent baking unit. A sizable pit, constructed for stoking the kiln through an arched opening at the base of the unit, left the lower chamber exposed. During the past month since Don Fernando's previous inspection, someone had smashed in a big portion of the unit and filled the stoking pit with rubbish. Our host said that he had unsuccessfully appealed for aid in protecting the site. It would therefore be just a short time until these 2000-year-old traces of another civilization vanished forever. As we stood looking in disgust at what was occurring at this one spot, we lamented this common worldwide disgrace. Not merely due to lack of funds but also because of sheer ignorance, man is recklessly eradicating his own past.

The Roman kiln was still very much on our minds the following morning as we visited the largest workshop in Triana, Seville's ancient potters' quarters. In the midst of a veritable warren of cubicles, scaffoldings, stairwells, grinding bins, and heaps of unfinished and discarded objects—all of which were covered with moss-like streamers of the soot and powdery dust that result from working clay—were two large kilns exactly like their Roman prototypes. The shop's wooden structures crowded in so tightly around the kilns that we were amazed that the whole place had not burned down long ago. Underscored by the relative scarcity of wood that could be used for fuel in this part of the province, the kilns demonstrated an extraordinary continuity of a cultural trait.

Our long, drawn-out studies in southern Spain came to an unforgettable conclusion on the last day of this refresher trip. We were invited to represent the hotel where we had been staying for the month at some sort of a gala sponsored by the local office of tourism. We were told that a *coche antigua* would pick us up that evening to take us to an unknown hall where the program would take place.

We assumed that our mode of transit would be one of the many horse-drawn buggies that conspicuously carry tourists about the city. To our surprise, our conveyance that evening turned out to be a highly polished 1926 Ford touring car with its canvas top down. Our driver and his wife, members of Seville's antique automobile club, were dressed in 1920s finery and were out to have a good time. The husband, a jocular, friendly natural goodwill ambassador, told us that it was appropriate for us to be riding in his car as he pointed to the Ford emblem and said "U-sa". We finally interpreted that as being U.S.A. We nodded in agreement that it was just right, as our automobile joined a procession of a dozen old cars carrying foreign guests from other hotels. For half an hour we toured the narrow streets of the heart of the old sector, our horns blaring and all of us waving to the surprised and smiling crowds of shoppers that were clogging the area during the early evening. It was great fun, made even sweeter when we learned that our destination was to be the Alcázar, a building that was located next to the cathedral and was considered to be the most revered Sevillian monument.

The original Alcázar, or fort, had been erected upon Roman foundations by twelfth-century Almohads and backed up against a massive rammed earthen wall that encircled their metropolis. After the Almohads were driven back to Morocco during the middle of the thirteenth century, the building had continued to serve as the living quarters for the conquering Christian rulers whenever their mobile courts took up residence in Andalusia. During the reign of Peter the Cruel in the 1360s, extensive remodeling and additions had made it into a *mudéjar* residence of large, high-ceilinged rooms surrounding interior courtyards. Many local potters had found employment by making the Alcázar's earthenware, ranging from drain pipes to roof and floor tiles. The rich ornamentation of carved stucco and tiled mosaics resembled that of the contemporaneous Alhambra located 130 miles to the east, but the feeling of a solid fortified edifice rather than of a delicate pleasure palace remained.

During the time of the devout Isabella and Ferdinand and about the same time that overseas Spaniards had spread out from the Caribbean islands onto the American mainland, an altar was erected in one small side chamber. Hanging above the altar was an Adoration scene that had been made of large, smooth-surfaced polychrome tiles by an Italian artist who had just recently moved to Seville. Toward the end of the century, other migrant Italians then living in the city followed the same stylistic mode to create panels of such tiles for a gallery at the rear of the Alcázar.

Some of the Almohad defensive walls and all of the tiled rooms had been preserved and were open to the public during daylight hours. We had viewed them on several occasions, but this time was special. Strategically placed spotlights warming the façades imparted a glowing quality to the formal structure that was absent during the harsher light of day. The grime of centuries faded in the darkness, leaving points of beauty dramatized as if on a stage. We were seated in an expansive atrium before one wing of the building, where we were joined by many local dignitaries and their ladies to be entertained by a symphony orchestra. Not quite able to believe that I was really in such a historical place under these enjoyable circumstances, I sat spellbound by the melodious music filling the balmy night air, absentmindedly watching disturbed bats flit up and down the darkened passageways. After several speeches about the incomparable Andalusian touristic charms and introductions of the guests from many countries, we all filed into an inner court where long tables awaited us, filled with luscious *tapas*, the justly famous Jérez sherry, the ever-present sangría, and the thirst-quenching San Miguel beer. As Bob moved off arm-in-arm with our jolly driver to sample this repast, I stepped back into the shadows. I needed a few moments alone to impress this spectacle upon my mind forever.

Watching the happy crowd milling about or sitting at small tables arranged around a bubbling central fountain with soft music playing in the background, I could not help but think that this was probably very much the way the palace would have looked in the past when it had been occupied and when finely dressed courtiers had gathered for a celebration. After all, it had been a home where royalty was born, married, lived out parts of their lives, and eventually died. A party in progress humanized an otherwise coldly sterile pile. Perhaps Isabella—she who had sanctioned Columbus's dream—had stood then where I was standing now. How had she reacted to this daily reminder of her vanquished adversaries' aesthetical prowess, which was also an expression of its craftsmen's intense religiosity? Had her tiny shrine with its tiled Adoration scene represented a subconscious need to affirm her own fervent beliefs in the face of this engulfing Islamization? My musings brought me back to the structure itself and to the realization that its adornment had undergone a remarkable nighttime transformation. Soft lights danced off the texture of the sculptured plaster of upper walls, creating deep valleys of shadow that visually thrust raised surfaces toward the viewer. The running yards of tile wainscoting, cool by day as befitted a warm climate, at night were sensually aglow in their gleaming smoothness. Vivid in solid primary colors and laid in complex, intertwined patterns with no beginning and no end, the panels mellowed into a satiny tapestry.

Almost caressingly, I am sure, I passed a hand over one such dado at my side. Over a shoulder I heard a man say, "It is beautiful, no"? as he passed by to replenish his glass. Thoughtfully to myself, I responded, "Yes, quite." In my reverie my mind flashed from the coarse, pinched-coil Anasazi pot made to hold a corn gruel that had ignited my youthful curiosity to this almost overwhelming climax of *mudéjar* ceramic magic meant to bedazzle the beholder and remind him or her that there is no God but Allah. What more glorious end to an enduring affair of the mind and heart?

THE SERIOUS SIDE

Had we tried, we could never have found a body of ceramics so fissured with global history as that of Spain's. Almost universal in the scope of its potential for the exploration of technological, economical, social, and religious aspects of societies that were separated by otherwise impenetrable barriers of time and space, its massive dimensions made my initial studies of Anasazi pottery seem almost paltry.

Spanish-tradition pottery drew from the ceramic wisdom of Classicism as interpreted by a Muslim world that stretched from Persia to Morocco, who in turn had absorbed technical and decorative surges from China and then passed on the composite craft to the western brink of Europe. Over time, necessary raw materials from various parts of the continent, such as tin from Cornwall and cobalt from Saxony, had brought others into the orbit of pottery production in al Andalus. Just as the lengthy tradition seemed on the brink of extinction during the sixteenth century, however, Italian donors, themselves heirs to the ceramic knowledge of Islam, injected new life and Renaissance themes into it, thereby ensuring its survival. This complex amalgam of pottery-associated traits had then come to the Americas as part of the transplanted Spanish cultural complex. There, midway between East and West, it had been impacted further by a flood of ideas derived from Chinese porcelain to emerge as a distinctive Mexican statement. The wares resulting from that activity had subsequently been distributed from Venezuela to California as the tentacles of the

Alicatado fragmented tile typical of Andalusian Muslim craftsmanship

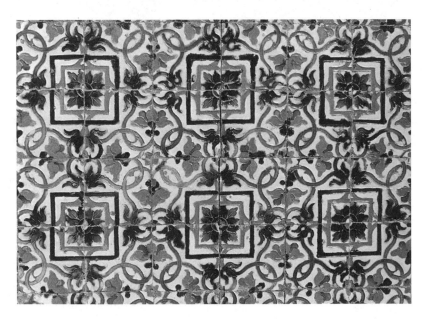

Renaissance-style square tile introduced in the sixteenth century to southern Spain by migrant Italian artisans

Spanish Empire reached out across the Western Hemisphere. In the first piece of maiolica I ever saw—a partial plate taken from the *convento* at Pecos Pueblo in New Mexico—there were therefore Muslim know-how, Spanish lace, Mexican craftsmanship, and Ming blue-on-white palette.

My ceramic analysis was based upon provenience data as well as upon the stylistic features of the workmanship levels, the forms, the sizes, the qualities, and the colors of glazes and decorations. Chemists at the Smithsonian Institution, headed by Jacqueline S. Olin, substantiated the distinctions that I had found in my studies between the late fifteenth- and early sixteenth-century wares exported from Spain to the Indies and to New Spain and those that I regarded as later Mexican copies of them. They also found that Mexican clays generally contained volcanic inclusions, whereas Spanish clays did not.

From its beginnings, the Spanish ceramic craft was far removed from an activity of a few women seated outside their doors hand-coiling ropes of clay to form domestic cooking and serving vessels, baking them in nearby smoky heaps, and then putting them to use in their households. Instead, Spanish ceramics represented commercial enterprises whose male employees had specialized in using molds or kick wheels to fashion thousands of identical objects whose shapes, sizes, and decorative modes were dictated by overseerers or craft guilds in accordance with the established canons of taste. Their products had been finished in two-chambered, updraft kilns capable of achieving temperatures twice as high as those of open firings. It was big business as opposed to cottage industries. The resulting products had then been sold either in bulk to merchants as housewares or as coarse packaging for various dry or liquid commodities, or by the piece to individuals.

On the social level, an appraisal of pottery shapes turned out by Andalusian and Spanish colonial artisans provides a fascinating register of lifestyles through the ages. Some utilitarian forms were obviously so well-suited for their intended purposes that they remained unaltered for centuries. These include the amphora, the spouted water jar, the water wheel jar, the olive jar, the brazier, and the canteen. Other shapes, however, reflected social change. Oil lamps gave way to candleholders, and large communal serving bowls were augmented by individual porringers. In their own ways, drug jars, chamber pots, baptismal fonts, inkwells, holy water stoups, and condiment dishes each tell something about life as it was at different periods of time.

Oil paintings, guild records, medical treatises, business accounts, and government documents allow faces to be put on an artisan class that typically has remained anonymous. We have been able to learn of its health hazards; its labor organizations; its financial troubles; its dowries; its religious obligations; and its racial, class, and religious prejudices. And finally, we have come to know of the export of wares and of the emigration of potters to the New World.

REFERENCES

Lister, Florence C. and Robert H. Lister. "Majolica, Ceramic Link Between Old World and New," *El Palacio,* No. 76, 1–15, 1969.

———. "Making Majolica Pottery in Modern Mexico." *El Palacio,* No. 78, 21–32, 1972.

———. "Maiolica in Colonial Spanish America." *Historical Archaeology,* No. 8, 17–52, 1974.

———. "An Overview of Moroccan Maiolica. Collected Papers in Honor of Florence Hawley Ellis." *Papers of the Archaeological Society of New Mexico,* No. 2, 272–95, 1975.

———. "Non-Indian Ceramics from the Mexico City Subway." *El Palacio,* No. 81, 25–48, 1975b.

———. "Distribution of Mexican Maiolica Along the Northern Borderlands. Collected Papers in Honor of Marjorie Ferguson Lambert." *Papers of the Archaeological Society of New Mexico,* No. 3, 113–40, 1976.

———. *A Descriptive Dictionary for 500 Years of Spanish-Tradition Ceramics (13th Through 18th Centuries).* Special Publication, No. 1, Society for Historical Archaeology, 100 pp., 1976b.

———. "The First Mexican Maiolicas: Imported and Locally Produced." *Historical Archaeology,* No. 10, 28–41, 1978.

———. "The Recycled Pots and Potsherds of Spain." *Historical Archaeology,* No. 15, 66–78, 1981.

———. "Sixteenth Century Maiolica Pottery in the Valley of Mexico." *Anthropological Papers of the University of Arizona,* No. 39, 110 pp., 1982.

———. "One Pot's Pedigree. Collected Papers in Honor of Charlie R. Steen." *Papers of the Archaeological Society of New Mexico,* No. 8, 167–87, 1983.

———. "The Potter's Quarter of Colonial Puebla, Mexico." *Historical Archaeology,* No. 18, 87–102, 1984.

———. *Andalusian Ceramics in Spain and New Spain: A Cultural Register from the Third Century B.C. to 1700.* University of Arizona Press, Tucson, 411 pp., 1987.

To conclude our lengthy review of Spanish-tradition ceramics, we donated our extensive sherd study collection to the University of Florida, where Kathleen Deagan and her students are engaged in related studies. Thus it joined that of John Goggin, who blazed a trail that we followed and expanded. Such is the way of scholarship. The following plaque made it all worthwhile.

THE LISTER COLLECTION
OF SPANISH CERAMICS

In Recognition and Appreciation
Of the Pioneering Research by
FLORENCE AND ROBERT LISTER
Into Spanish Colonial Material Life,
Culture, and Social History.
The Lister Collection
Will Allow
Many Future Generations of Scholars
To Benefit From and Share
In Their Rich Contributions
To Historical Archaeology.
Florida Museum of Natural History
University of Florida
February 14, 1990

About Bob

What started out as my story obviously cannot be left as that, for my adult life was a valued partnership with a caring man named Robert Hill Lister. It was a partnership that had little, yet everything, to do with my own hit-and-miss pursuit of ceramic knowledge.

Unlike many of his colleagues who had been lured to the Southwest from elsewhere, Bob was proud of being a native son of New Mexico, born in Las Vegas on August 7, 1915. His early school years were spent in southern California, but during many summers his parents had put him on the Santa Fe Railroad, tipped a porter to look after him, and sent him to the ranch of his maternal grandparents near Watrous, now virtually a tiny ghost town that was designated as a National Historical Landmark during the taking of the West.

The ranch was a sprawling cow outfit headquartered amid a lush meadow-land that was flushed by broad irrigation ditches and shaded by huge cotton-woods and willow thickets. Out in the distance was a rolling prairie pasture as green as a lawn in good years. The main house, built in the 1870s by Tennessean William Tipton for his sixteen-year-old bride, was a two-story adobe. Many of its fourteen high-ceilinged rooms had fireplaces, and it was faced by a façade of double-decked white columns. This pseudo-Southern style suited the large Hill family, who, after purchasing the property, from about 1910 seasonally came west from Mississippi to experience life on what they considered to be the frontier.

From the 1850s through the 1870s the Mountain Branch of the Santa Fe Trail that cut through the yard was the main highway connecting nearby Fort Union to the territorial capital of Santa Fe. On occasion the Hills, whose ancestors had fought with the Confederacy during the Civil War, rode across their pasture to prowl through the empty shells of officers' quarters at that Union outpost. The house that had stood by the side of the Trail burned down in the 1960s, and there were only stubby foundations and hardy lilac bushes that had been planted by Grandmother Hill left standing to mark its location. The Trail itself remained an eroded path leading down to the junction of the Mora and Sapello Rivers, where the stage stop of Fort Barclay had been erected in the 1840s.

A massive stone quadrangle spread along the western side of the shallow ruts. During the Trail's heyday and the establishment of Fort Union, it had become a stopping place that offered water and stables for livestock; and meals, lodging, and protection from marauding Indians for weary travelers. During the Hill tenancy, the structure had become a corral and a workshop. Under a heavy smear of grime and dust the name "Bobby" and the date of his arrival remain scratched into the wood, carved by the old Mexican blacksmith who had worked for Grandfather Hill.

Bob's constant companion during his summers on the Clyde Ranch (named for the Clydesdale horses that were bred there) was a devoted bachelor uncle who taught him how to ride horses, brand cattle, carry out a myriad of ranch chores, and be at ease with life in the open and with the folks who worked the land. From the Mexican laborers who lived in the village of Tiptonville, then part of the ranch holdings, and were sustained by a venerable patronage system, he acquired a coarse country Spanish; an insatiable appetite for hot, biting chile; and an abiding interest in Hispanic culture as it was mutated on this northern shore of the vanquished Spanish empire. He was on such good terms with the Mexican workers that they permitted him to observe their secret Easter *penitente* rituals at a tiny *morada* up canyon from the ranch. For the first time in his life, he was also exposed to Indian lore when on Sunday outings, he and his family clambered into the tumbled remains of old dwellings that were silently falling apart in alcoves scattered through the vicinity, or scoured the pastures, picking up the stone remains from some passing native bands. Certainly these varied experiences coming during his most formative years had slowly molded Bob's future. Unlike my own abrupt introduction to the undercurrents of Southwestern life, his background had slowly built his personality like some geological stratum.

During the hard Depression years, the family patriarch, Joseph Hill, who had once been the wealthy owner of an antebellum home on the Mississippi Gulf Coast, a bank in Gulfport, and a lumber mill in the pine woods, had lost his extensive fortune before he died. His widow (Minnie Pearl, honest!), his sons, and an unmarried daughter then hunkered down on the Clyde Ranch. They soon were joined by his eldest daughter, her husband, and their son Bob. Bob transferred from Hollywood High School to Las Vegas High, where he graduated in 1933. Determined that her son should go to college and join a Southern-allied fraternity as she thought proper, Mother Bye became a teacher in the one-room school in Watrous in order to earn his tuition money. Bob and his father packed lettuce in a processing shed in Colorado's San Luis Valley, and in his spare time, Bob's father Frank initiated lobbying efforts to have Fort Union set aside as a national monument.

At the University of New Mexico Bob was active in campus life, became president of his fraternity, and was elected to the senior mens' honorary society, which pleased his mother. He also earned annual athletic letters in track, setting several Border Conference records in the broad jump and in the 100-yard dash, which pleased his father. He had intended to study architecture, but soon realized that he had little ability in mathematics. That is when he gravitated to the young Department of Anthropology that had been established by Edgar L. Hewett, then a giant in regional studies. With his letterman's sweaters, fraternity ring, and sorority girl friends, Bob did not fit the then-current image of the department's students as nonconformists in both dress and conduct. Nevertheless, he was at the center of action during his college years. He attended the archaeological field school at Jemez Springs that was directed by Hewett. He participated in the excavation of the Paleo-Indian remains at Sandia Cave and earned thirty-five cents an hour drawing stratigraphic profiles for Frank Hibben's report. He studied Indian art with Kenneth Chapman. He helped Paul Goodbear, a Plains Indian then in the department, in reclaiming and recording the fifteenth-century kiva murals at the site of Kuaua, where Coronado is thought to have spent the winter of 1540–41. During several summers, he also joined field parties to northern and central Mexico, and one to central Utah.

One professor who had a great influence on Bob was Donald D. Brand, freshly graduated from the University of California with a degree in anthropogeogra-

*Lab crew at University of New Mexico Jemez Springs archaeological field school,
1935. Marge Lambert, director, at right; Bob Lister, student helper, at left*

phy and a passion for Latin American studies. Brand, having an encyclopedic
mind that stored voluminous hard facts and inconsequential trivia like a modern computer, was a relentless taskmaster as a teacher, since he expected his
students to have the same capabilities. Classroom encounters were further complicated by his rapid-fire delivery in a mixture of English and Spanish with
both languages having decidedly peculiar phonologies. The student consensus
was that since Brand's parents had been missionaries to Peru, his nanny there
may have been an Indian who handled neither language well. Even with those
obstacles, however, Brand inspired such an interest in the convoluted prehistory of central Mexico that for years Bob contemplated making it the center-
piece of his own research. The last time the two met was at the 1970 annual
meeting of the Society for American Archaeology held in Mexico City, at which
time Bob assumed the presidency of the organization. The Listers arranged a
luncheon for Brand, but already approaching dotage, he forgot to come.

Another of Bob's mentors was Florence Hawley. Although scarcely older
than he, she continued to address him as "my dear boy" even as they both
aged. She had yet to obtain her Ph.D. degree, but she was already establishing

Donald Brand at work in central Mexico, 1939

a reputation for herself in ceramic analysis, dendrochronology, Anasazi archaeology, and Pueblo ethnology. Florence joined the university faculty in 1934,
and Bob enrolled in her first class. Years later he still felt indebted to her for
having drilled into him the critical importance of knowing something about
the lifestyles of the modern Native Americans in the northern Southwest, so
that he could attempt to interpret their presumed roots.

There was a clubby atmosphere within the small anthropology department
of perhaps three dozen persons, which put staff and students on a first-name
basis that was quite at odds with the usual reserved dichotomy between those
who were and those who hoped to be. Being young, unmarried, and eager to
fit into her new surroundings, Florence soon had a circle of followers. Bob was
one of them. On many weekends with her coterie in tow, Florence took the
opportunity of making friends with the people living in the Indian villages
near Albuquerque. She found some of the families at the Zia Pueblo to be par-

ticularly friendly. It therefore became a Sunday morning ritual for the Hawley contingency to show up with old phonograph records or abalone and other kinds of shells, which the native craftsmen wanted for making jewelry, and barter with them for pots and baskets. For a mollusk picked up on the beach at Laguna or Torrey Pines on the Pacific Coast, with perhaps a U.S. quarter thrown in, one could acquire an item that would in future years become a treasure. A seed of compulsive acquisition was firmly planted in Florence during these casual encounters, and this trait eventually led to an extensive museum-quality collection of Indian and Spanish Colonial arts and crafts that overflowed her various homes throughout the years. Being on the scene at a propitious time with good taste and her pocketbook at the ready paid off handsomely.

During one spring break Bob drove the two of them to Miami, Arizona, where Florence's parents lived in dreary company housing and Mr. Hawley was employed as a chemist for the copper smelter there. There Bob witnessed a warm relationship between Florence and her father, who had written a paper together on the composition of pigments used by Southwestern Indian potters. The relationship was strained, however, between Florence and her mother, whose rigid beliefs had once denied her college-age daughter the chance of attending the first Pecos Conference because she lacked a chaperone. One can only imagine her later maternal distress at having her only daughter choose to be married out in the middle of nowhere within the looming broken walls of the Quarai Mission, even though Florence's friend, Bob Lister, did sweep out the drifts of windborne dirt and decorate the aisle with juniper branches. On the other hand, she must have approved of the bride's floor-length white wedding gown even as its hem turned brown in the dust.

In the summer of 1936, Bob secured a job as camp boy for the archaeological field school that was set up in tents pitched within the abandoned Richard Wetherill ranch compound at Chaco Canyon. Another camp boy was Alden Hayes, who was to remain one of Bob's lifelong friends and be his coworker at Chaco at the end of both of their careers. Bob threw his bedroll down onto the floor of the cook tent so that he could arise at four in the morning and get the fires going in the wood stoves that were presided over by two Indian women who were fond of a nip from the bottle and were given to taking after smart-tongued students with their butcher knives. Every week Bob also maneuvered the derelict camp truck over the tortuous rutted track down to U.S. 66 and on

Florence Hawley Senter, Quarai Mission, 1936

to Gallup in order to purchase supplies. Once the truck broke in half on the way back, with the cab plunged downward into one set of furrows and the bed plunged backward into another. Hours later on that moonless soggy night, Bob limped into camp with the two truck sections tenuously lashed together in time to build the cookfires, but with the blocks of ice that were vital for preservation and for drinks nothing but puddles. In retrospect, however, it was not these part-of-the-job activities that were to bring Bob his widest recognition.

Without Bob's prior knowledge, Brand, a former track man himself, arranged a foot race between his student and a young Navajo who was also considered to be a good runner. In those days, there were a number of Navajo families living in and near the treeless outlands of Chaco Canyon, and this event promised to be a welcome novel diversion for everyone. Betting was heavy on both sides, as Brand took charge of a kitty of crumpled dollar bills and pieces of silver-and-turquoise jewelry. An old photograph shows some three dozen Navajo men sitting on horseback or squatting beside what was to be the track in the bottom of Escavada Wash. Neither participant had proper outfits; so each ran

Foot race in Chaco Canyon before Navajo spectators, 1936. Bob Lister at left

barefoot in his undershorts. The going through the loose sand was slow, but in the end, Bob won. The honor of the field school was saved, and Bob's status with his professor and with all those who had risked their spending money was protected. One winner was John Corbett, later Chief Archeologist for the National Park Service and Bob's predecessor in that job. John won a silver bracelet that he wore until the day he died. The Chaco race became a bit of folklore that followed Bob around like a shadow for the rest of his life, a story that was retold for the last time at his final memorial service.

After obtaining a Master of Arts degree in 1938, Bob was one of the lucky ones to get employment in his chosen field. He signed on as Ranger-Archeologist in the National Park Service. His first assignment was at Bandelier National Monument northwest of Santa Fe, where he was hired to work on the Tyuoni site.

Dating back to the fifteenth and sixteenth centuries, Tyuoni and a separate series of small rooms were banked up against a cliff wall and spread through a narrow valley along the Rio de los Frijoles that flowed off the evergreen Pajarito Plateau. Beginning in 1907 and continuing for a number of years, the sites were partially dug or tested by the Southwest's first field training school, which was directed by Edgar Hewett. Earl Morris and Jesse Nusbaum, two pioneers in the archaeology of the northern area, were among its participants. Even though the ruins had been included in the Bandelier National Monument in 1916, they were left open after excavation and quickly deteriorated.

In the mid-1930s the National Park Service began to remedy that situation as part of a large-scale development program. A dirt road was cut down a cliff side to replace the creaking tramway that had formerly been used to bring in supplies and baggage. Civilian Conservation Corps crews erected thirty-two stone buildings to be used as a lodge, an administrative center, and housing for the staff; and they also made the furnishings for the buildings. Pablita Velarde, a twenty-year-old Santa Clara artist, was commissioned to paint murals for a new museum. Concessionaires George and Evelyn Frey prepared for visitors. Bob was hired to clean up Tyuoni and excavate those rooms in Long House that had not yet been opened. He accomplished these tasks with the help of Civilian Conservation Corps workers, whose practical jokes made life miserable for "the college kid" who was their own age.

His next assignment took Bob to Casa Grande National Monument in southern Arizona. Afterward in the spring of 1940, he returned to Chaco Canyon National Monument, where our paths almost crossed that summer. Two memorable events transpired during that Chaco stint. One day after Bob had guided two elderly men through the great masonry complex of Pueblo Bonito, the younger man introduced the older fellow as his father, William Henry Jackson. Bob was stunned to meet the West's pioneer photographer who had first come to Chaco Canyon in 1877. During this return visit, the Jacksons requested that Bob lead them up the cliff behind Pueblo Bonito, so that they could view the site from above. Bob was honored to oblige. He took the son, who was in his seventies, and the legendary father, then ninety-seven years old, up a steep, badly worn aboriginal stairway to the rim several hundred feet above the site for what probably was to be a final viewing for them both.

The other occurrence also involved the high cliff behind Pueblo Bonito. At its crest a pair of iron bars were projected opposite a matching pair that had been pounded into the top of a massive vertical monolith. The monolith had broken free from the mother cliff long before the Anasazi built their community of Pueblo Bonito at its feet, and a wide crevice yawned between the matrix cliff and the free-standing slab. Named Threatening Rock by the park personnel because it looked as if it would come crashing down at any moment onto the hundreds of rooms below, the massive rock formation showed signs of weakening or tilting outward. Bob was therefore given the unnerving task of measuring the gap between the pairs of rods twice a day in an attempt to detect any movement by Threatening Rock. A faded snapshot taken by the monument custodian shows Bob, who was lying prone on his stomach with a fellow ranger sitting on his outstretched legs and precariously reaching out from the cliff toward Threatening Rock to take these readings. Although some of his Navajo friends teased him about it, I never knew whether to believe that he had actually jumped over onto the upper surface of Threatening Rock several times. After all, he had been a skillful broad jumper. The huge, isolated chunk of sandstone actually did fall in January 1941, crushing the highest portion of the ruin. One Navajo is said to have seen it collapse, and he was so frightened by the experience that he ran for his horse and raced out of the canyon, never to be seen again. Or so the story goes.

The Vivian family befriended Bob during his Chaco tenure. At their large hogan on the south side of the canyon, Myrtle frequently prepared heaping plates of flat, red chile enchiladas for the three of them while Gordon held forth on his decade of experiences with the antiquities and with the resident Native Americans. To the group's delight, he surely embroidered upon the time he had rescued that foolhardy blond who thought she could take a car where even stalwart men hesitated to go!

Gordon Vivian first went to Chaco Canyon in 1928 as a driver for Edgar Hewett, director of the Museum of New Mexico who had established the Department of Anthropology at the state university just a year earlier. He returned the next several summers to participate in excavations at Chetro Ketl, the second largest house block in the canyon. That learning period had been followed by a second student project, clearing the isolated Great Kiva of Casa Rinconada. From the mid-1930s to the mid-1950s Vivian directed a crew of Navajo workmen for the National Park Service in the delicate task of making needed repairs to various parts of the old structures while keeping those measures as inconspicuous as possible. In a program that extended over twenty years, he trained the workers to be skilled masons; taught them to write their names so that they could sign payrolls; counciled them when asked; drove them or their families to the Crownpoint clinic when necessary; and on occasion, buried their dead. When stabilization or salvage required excavation, he—as Richard Wetherill and Neil Judd had done long before him—oversaw a crew of modern Native Americans in unearthing the discards of others who had made Chaco Canyon their home centuries earlier.

Ultimately Gordon Vivian was to live in Chaco Canyon for twenty-five years, which was longer than any other white man has done before or since. He spent much of this time alone when his family moved to town for schooling. The utter silence that enveloped the abandoned places like a shroud, the predictable seasonal and astronomical rhythms that came and went as they had for an eternity, and the total immersion in his work without any distractions combined to foster in this solitary, sensitive man a kind of mystical connection to the distant past. A person with practical manual skills and a firm commitment to objective archaeological science, he was also acutely attuned to the invisible spirits that haunt the ghost towns of Chaco and continue even today to draw New Agers with their drums and crystals. Gordon's son Gwinn once wrote movingly of witnessing his father's reaction to the sudden devastation caused by a flash flood that ripped through Chetro Ketl, dislodging roof timbers, knocking walls awry, and paving the courtyard with many feet of tumbled debris. Obviously shaken at the sight before him but not saying a word, Gordon strode rapidly to his truck and disappeared for the day to grieve alone over the violation of a community that held special meaning for him.

In the spring of 1941, when Bob was teaching at the university and we had decided to build a life together, our world crumbled around us. One week Bob was notified that he had been awarded a predoctoral fellowship at Harvard University that had been set up by New Mexico Senator Bronson Cutting to give poor local men a taste of Ivy League culture. The next week, however, his Selective Service number was drawn in Albuquerque's first draft lottery. Harvard agreed to hold the fellowship until he had fulfilled his military obligation, and the Draft Board granted him a deferment through the summer so that he could join Brand for another excavation in central Mexico.

Upon Bob's return from Mexico, he gave me a large diamond ring that had once belong to his Grandmother Hill. As we came out of the jewelry store where the ring had been sized, the first person we met was Dr. Florence. When we told her about our engagement, she smiled, patted me on the shoulder, and said, "He's just the fellow I had in mind for you!"

In September Bob was inducted into the army at the old armory in Santa Fe. As he stood apprehensively in line, a sergeant, seated at a table piled high with the prerequisite government forms, asked in a bored voice flattened by endless repetition, "Soldier, what did you do in civilian life?"

"I'm an archaeologist," Bob replied.

That got the sergeant's attention.

"What the hell is that?" he growled as he finally looked up at the man whose future he was determining.

"Well, we dig . . ." was as far as Bob got.

"Dig? Foxholes! Infantry! Next!"

And so it was to be the Infantry for the next four years.

Bob's basic training was almost over when Pearl Harbor was bombed and his company was shipped to California to prepare to go to the South Pacific. The night before his troop ship was to sail, orders came through assigning Bob to Officers' Candidate School. Therefore, his possessions went to Guadalcanal, while he went to Fort Benning, Georgia. During a ten-day delay en route, he almost died in an Albuquerque hospital from a case of Rocky Mountain spotted fever that he had apparently acquired from a tick bite while on coastal patrol duty. A vaccination some years earlier when he had joined a field party in Utah led by John Gillen may have saved his life.

Wearing new Second Lieutenant's bars, Bob stayed for a year at the Infantry School to teach map reading and aerial photo interpretation, both skills that were needed by archaeologists as well as by soldiers. Jubilant with what seemed to be a windfall of security in such turbulent times, we married on a sweltering July day in 1942 at the historic George Washington Christ Church in Alexandria, Virginia, where just a short time before our visit Franklin Roosevelt and Winston Churchill had worshipped. With Bob's parents, whom I had met just the day before, looking on, I was baptized and then became a war bride within less than an hour.

Ultimately Bob joined a newly formed division that was sent to the European Theater of Operations. The Battle of the Bulge occurred while their convoy was in the mid-Atlantic, causing Bob once again to be parted from his gear. It docked in England. He docked in France. The war's end found him in Czechoslovakia. The Army of Occupation then took him to the Bavarian Nazi concentration camp of Dachau where he helped to clean up the carnage that had occurred there. Finally on Thanksgiving Day 1945, Bob came home, having the rank of Major and a Bronze Star.

Bob seldom talked about his war experiences, except to tell of the only time he had met his commanding officer. One day General George Patton abruptly stopped his motorcade beside the open Jeep in which Bob was seated.

"Captain," he shouted, "put that Goddamn top up!"

"Yes, sir!" Salute. And the leader of the troops roared into the distance.

Back at Harvard, Bob was awed by the personalities behind such names as Kidder, Brew, Tozzer, Coon, Scott, and Hooton, then very prominent in American anthropology. Kluckhohn was already Bob's advisor because of their previous association in New Mexico. Nonetheless, because of the war's interruption, Bob felt pressured to get out of school and off on his own. He therefore took a full course load for credit and simultaneously audited a full load. We divided his long required reading list so that I could outline books for him. At the end of one academic year, he completed his residency and passed his comprehensives. It was a formidable feat then and would be impossible now.

To Tozzer's dismay, Bob turned down a job in the Mayan field in Honduras to accept an instructorship at the University of Colorado. It was such a lowly position that before long it was abolished, but it meant that we could come back home with Frank, our own new contribution to the Boomer Generation.

Bob easily settled into the academic routine. He enjoyed teaching and always considered it to be his forte. When asked about his occupation, he would invariably answer, "Oh, I'm just an old school teacher." The pay was low compared to some other professions, but there were rewards in helping several generations of students and enjoying the special bond that was created by shared experiences off campus, both good and not so good. His military responsibilities had given him the managerial skills that he later used for a dozen years when he became a department chairman. The athletic programs at the university and public schools afforded him some needed recreation. For many years he was head timer for the university track meets, and he quite intentionally passed on to his two sons his love for competitive sports. Early archaeological field work took him to northern and western Colorado and to southern Utah.

Mexican antiquities continued to fascinate him, but after a decade he found that political and family considerations had made working there difficult. He then concentrated for ten seasons on directing a summer field school and re-search center at Mesa Verde National Park. Under his leadership, four house blocks and the Mummy Lake Reservoir in the Far View group were excavated, and several villages as well as the Great Kiva in Morefield Canyon were tested. Off the mesa, Bob negotiated for excavation or stabilization of sites in what was to become the Ute Mountain Ute Tribal Park, in Chimney Rock, in Es-calante Ruin, and in Lowry Ruin, all of which were located in southwestern Colorado.

By the late 1960s, however, Bob had become restless. He was distressed at the campus unrest that he saw within both the faculty and the student body. He sensed that the brand of historical-descriptive archaeology, which he had been taught and had practiced for three decades, was becoming outdated as the discipline built on that base moved into a more conceptual phase. He did not have a theoretical turn of mind, and he desperately wanted a change.

That opportunity came when the National Park Service asked him to plan and direct a long-term project that focused on Chaco Canyon and its ancient culture. He was pleased because he had begun his career with this branch of the government, serving as a collaborator on projects at Dinosaur National Monument, Colorado National Monument, and Mesa Verde National Park; and he respected the organization's contributions to the educational and recreational benefit of the public. The appointment also included an adjunct professorship at his alma mater, the University of New Mexico. His return to scenes that brought so many memories was a joyful one. Although he did not realize it at the time, however, his days as a teacher and researcher were numbered. He soon became a full-time administrator, a position he knew to be critical in fa-cilitating the work of others who were using the burgeoning new refinements. He was also pleased that his son Gary was putting his photographic expertise to work in the Chaco Center Remote Sensing Section during his graduate stud-ies at the university.

Shortly thereafter, at the urging of Emil Haury, a respected colleague and friend of long standing, Bob reluctantly took on a second bureaucratic job as

Chief Archeologist for the National Park Service. This meant regular commutes to Washington, tackling what seemed like endless personnel and budgetary problems and interrupting work that was much dearer to his heart. For these reasons, he resigned this position after eighteen months.

From 1976 to 1978, he organized and ran the Southwest Cultural Resource office in Santa Fe for the Park Service. By coincidence, many of his staff members had once been his students at the University of Colorado. One of his last projects again involved him with Bandelier National Monument, where it had all begun nearly forty years earlier, when a disastrous lightning-ignited fire required monitoring by his team of archaeologists. Then at last, he retired. He left his career as a man who was confidently at ease with himself because he had done what he wanted with his life and had been rewarded for it. He also had the satisfaction of seeing his two sons successfully launched in their own careers—Frank in tourism and Gary in business.

Retirement for Bob meant having the time to do the things that had long been percolating in the back of his mind. One of those projects was to co-author a series of books with me for the interested public on facets of Southwestern and Spanish Colonial archaeology. In a way this was a reflection of his commitment to the goals of the National Park Service, from whom he had received the Emil W. Haury award that was issued through the Southwest Parks and Monument Association.

Our working relationship was an easy one. When the topic was prehistory, Bob wrote a first draft. He would then typically hand it to me, saying, "Kiddo, jazz it up." I tried. When the subject matter was more historical, I did the archival searches and preliminary text, and Bob read that for accuracy and flow. The graphic art and photographs were Bob's responsibility, while I prepared the final copy, proofed the galleys, and compiled the indexes. Our wills did not clash, because each of us innately understood our individual contributions. It may seem medieval to the feminists, but for me, except in the area of ceramics, Bob had always been the master and I the apprentice. Had I earned a sheaf of degrees or been born thirty years later, I might have reacted differently. I make no apologies now for not feeling diminished by this attitude. Love, as they say, conquers all.

Between these creative endeavors, we traveled widely, sometimes to further our research interests and sometimes for pleasure. We also moved six times.

Finally we returned to the beautiful Mancos Valley in southwestern Colorado to build our nest in the rural territorial style of northern New Mexico, with a study window framing the majestic Mesa Verde.

Bob then started leading select archaeological tours to places of interest around the Four Corners. His long teaching experience and his stockpile of stories about the old days always made him a popular guide.

Our son Frank arranged one such trip, during which he, Bob, and the family of author Louis L'Amour camped for a night in a cliff dwelling in the Ute Mountain Ute Tribal Park. Louis elected to sleep on the floor of a kiva. The spirits must have reached him there because he soon wrote his metaphysical book, *Haunted Mesa*.

Another trip was organized by some Chicago area fans of Tony Hillerman, whom we had known at the University of New Mexico. One encounter during that time had been at the dedication of a new Albuquerque library, when the University Press asked the three of us to appear for a book-signing event. That evening we had sat at a table for hours without a single person coming to ask us for an autograph, but this time, it was different. We met at Chaco, then drove to the San Juan River, and finally returned to Mancos for a Mexican buffet at the Lister home. With his fans hanging onto his every word, Tony did a running monologue about his writing methods and about his novel, *The Thief of Time*, whose story line revolved around archaeologists at Chaco.

The final trip Bob led was for his Harvard friend Ned Danson, and the group also included some of Ned's nephews and his celebrity son Ted. On a crystalline day in May as the party was climbing out of Moon House—a lovely cliff-side structure mellowing in the solitude of southeastern Utah—and joking about anticipating a cold beer at rim top, Bob dropped dead.

This would surely have been that archaeologist's exit of choice.

ROBERT HILL LISTER,
1915–1990

Index